# Cybersecurity²

## Post-Secondary Graduate: Classroom to Employability

Clifton Ray Wise Ed.D.

Copyright © 2025 by Clifton Ray Wise.

All rights reserved. No part of this book may be reproduced or used in any manner without the prior written permission of the copyright owner, except for the use of brief quotations in a book review.

Author: Clifton Ray Wise Ed.D.

Epub : 979-8-9899236-6-3

Paperback : 979-8-9917742-1-5

Publisher: Clifton Ray Wise

# ACKNOWLEDGEMENTS

We like to think we are *self-made*, but in reality, no human entity is self-made, we are products of our environment, from when we are first brought into the light at birth until the day we draw our last breath and move to darkness.

In all of my previous writings I have acknowledged the human entities that have helped to make me who I am today. No one is in fact self-made. Every human entity on our planet is a culmination of their associations within their environment, good or bad. Some have good parental associations and there I have been lucky.

The older I become it occurs to me that some of us take more than a single hint to get a point across. I guess some of us are just stubborn that way, well, maybe the most of us. Remember when your parents didn't want to you to stay out late on a school night or didn't care for one of your friends. All that raced through your mind was: "You are just trying to hold me down from having fun". Remember any of that?

It took me 20, 30, and even 40 years to figure out: "They didn't want me to do the same stupid stuff they did, they wanted to save me from those same stupid mistakes! I call them learning experiences.

Learning experiences come in different levels depending upon the repercussions. Some are low level and some are high level! Some you can fix and some you cannot. Some are under YOUR control and some are not! Some are easy fixes and some are difficult.

This acknowledgement is for those who assist us with those learning experiences that make us who we are and who we strive to be.

When bad things happen to each of us, there are two human elements on this planet, which one do YOU want to be?

"I have always tried to do my best and why did this happen to me?"

OR

"I knew it was coming, it was a matter of time".

# PREFACE

This writing has been compiled as a means for professional development. I do not write for monetary gain, I write to help my students gain knowledge and expertise through my eyes within certain topics.

This writing is a culmination of information gathered through my term as a university professor of Computer Science. I have spent the majority of my years in industry, and I can assuredly tell you what industry wants and is looking for in a career applicant. There is a significant difference in a professor who progressed from K-12 student to professor, and the professor who later transitioned from industry to education.

I think the majority of difference is from the experiences gathered within those venues. I have found students to be more receptive if I offer up real-world experiences I have seen and been a part of, rather than just pointing at a textbook, reviewing slides, and giving assignments. I feel students get more of what you are saying if you can associate those ideas and concepts with anecdotes.

I feel the post-secondary classroom of today involves a lot of tangents. Today we have a majority student population derived from two distinct digital generations These students have different wants and needs than all past non-digital generations.

The topic of this writing is Cyber Security. My plan was not to write a mere book on Cyber Security but to take that topic as a base and add tangent ideas and concepts relative to the topic with the additions of education related laboratory activities, industry employability soft and hard skills, certifications and certificates, and a library of possible breaches.

If you remember little of the topic of Cybersecurity, always remember these:

100% security is a myth.

There is strength in numbers.

If there is a way out, there is a way in.

Have a little patience.

Do you kiss your mother with that mouth?

If you have a secret don't tell the town parrot.

Sometimes you just have to say "what the #@%$". (Fill it with YOUR interpretation)

# Table of Contents

**ACKNOWLEDGEMENTS** ................................................. I
**PREFACE** ................................................................... III
**INTRODUCTION** ........................................................ 5
**1...PREVIEW OF THINGS TO COME** ........................ 7
   Secure as Grandma's House ........................................... 7
   Defensive Provisions ....................................................... 8
   Research ......................................................................... 9
   Risk ............................................................................... 11
**2...FIRST THINGS FIRST** ........................................ 13
   Learning by Design ....................................................... 13
   Campus or Online ......................................................... 16
   Accreditations ............................................................... 17
   Will Anyone Hire Me? .................................................... 18
**3...'THINKING HATS'** ............................................... 21
   'Ten Gallon' the Critical Thinker .................................... 23
   'Sombrero' the Creative Thinker ................................... 28
   'Boonie' the Strategic Thinker ...................................... 41
   Seven Additional Hats .................................................. 44
      White Hard of the Manager ..................................... 45
      Fedora of the Conversant ....................................... 50
      Pith of the Explorer ................................................. 62
      Tam of the Scholar ................................................. 73
      Campaign of the Confident ..................................... 86

Propeller Beanie of the Happy ............................... 93
Dunce of the Labelled ............................................ 103

# 4...STOP, LOOK, AND LISTEN ............................... 111

When I was young ...................................................... 112
Think First .................................................................... 113
No Matter What ........................................................... 113

# 5...PENCILS AND PAPER ....................................... 115

Old Days Extended ..................................................... 116
Then Later ................................................................... 118

# 6...AS A STUDENT .................................................. 121

Become Involved ........................................................ 122
Research ..................................................................... 123
Due Diligence ............................................................. 124
Up to You .................................................................... 125

# 7...SOFT AND HARD SKILLS ................................. 129

# 8...CERTIFICATES OR CERTICICATIONS ............ 133

Years Ago ................................................................... 135
Currently ..................................................................... 136

# 9...PREPPING, GETTING, AND KEEPING ............ 139

Preparing… ................................................................. 139
Getting… ..................................................................... 140
Keeping… .................................................................... 141

# 10...SUCCESS IS UP TO YOU ................................ 143

# 11...MY CYBERSECURITY COURSE ACTIVITIES ..... 147

Discussions ................................................................. 147

- Oral/PowerPoints .................................................. 147
- Thinking Assignments ............................................ 147
- Essays ................................................................... 148
- Random Topics ..................................................... 148
  - Feeling Safe ..................................................... 148
  - Awareness ........................................................ 151
  - Car-Jacking ...................................................... 154
  - Drugging ........................................................... 155
  - Regrets ............................................................. 157
  - Struggles .......................................................... 159
  - Assaulting ......................................................... 161
  - Leader .............................................................. 163
  - Profiling ............................................................ 166
  - Assassination ................................................... 169
  - Eminent Domain ............................................... 173
  - Electronic Fraud ............................................... 178
  - Profiling II ......................................................... 179
  - Plagiarism ........................................................ 185
  - Disaster Recovery Plan (DRP) ......................... 187
  - Infrastructure ................................................... 189
  - Planning ........................................................... 192
  - Symbiotic ......................................................... 195
  - Respect ............................................................ 198
  - Research .......................................................... 202
  - Business Continuity Plan (BCP) ....................... 205
  - Assumptions .................................................... 207
  - Marketing ......................................................... 210
  - Death ............................................................... 214

- Bullying ............................................................. 217
- Suicide ............................................................... 222
- Last Year ........................................................... 226

## 12...MY ACTIVITY INSTRUCTIONS ............................ 231

- Discussion Instructions ................................... 231
- Oral/PowerPoint Instructions ......................... 232
- Thinking Assignment Instructions ................. 233
- Essay Instructions .......................................... 235

## 13...MY OTHER COURSE ACTIVITIES ....................... 237

- In the News .................................................... 237
- 5 Things I Learned ........................................ 237
- IT Field Technician ........................................ 238
- Pick a Software I ............................................ 242
- Pick a Cell App ............................................... 244
- A Helpful Document ...................................... 244
- Start a New Account ...................................... 246
- Cell Application I ............................................ 248
- Cell Application II ........................................... 249
- Cell Application III .......................................... 250

## ABOUT THE AUTHOR ............................................... 255

## NOTES ...................................................................... 257

# INTRODUCTION

This is a compilation of information related to security. Some of these topics may be a tangent, but they are all still quite relatable to security, or cyber security if you prefer the vastness of that as a relation. Virtually every avenue involving the human element has some relativity to security pre and post.

"It is important to understand the true definition of 'Cyber'. Cyber is a word relating to or characteristic of the culture of computers, information technology, and virtual technology. Typically characterized as "the cyber age". Cyber can be a prefix attached to any career designation that previously existed before 'the cyber age". Cyber is most often related to the Internet. The term "cyber" has become ingrained in our language and is commonly used to describe anything related to the digital realm, technology, and online communication."

Consider Cyber Security, Cyber Operations, or Cyber Forensics as your career path if you'd like to:

- **Defend** computer systems, networks, mobile devices, servers, electronic systems, data, and sensitive information against unauthorized access, illegal use, damage, and malicious attacks.
- **Protect** organizational assets from internal and external cyber-attacks and disruptions caused by natural disasters.
- **Ensure** confidentiality, integrity, and availability of information.

- **Learn** technologies, processes, methods, and controls to advance Cyber measures.

Sound like a plan? Sound like something YOU might like to become involved in to put you on the rails of a career path?

If YOU are interested? Within this writing there are bits of knowledge I will present to YOU.

# 1 ... PREVIEW OF THINGS TO COME

How about a brief scenario to see if you have interest. I call it "Secure as Grandma's House."

## Secure as Grandma's House

Think about the security of a house. A house is ONLY as secure as YOU make it. How much does it mean to you? How much protection are you willing to give? What is the level of risk?

Risk is relative to insurance. The assessment you give for your assets in relation to the insurance you provide to keep those assets from being compromised.

If you own a Volkswagen car you will not pay the insurance premium of a Porsche! Or will YOU? What is the replacement cost of the Volkswagen in comparison of the Porsche?

Back to the house…………..

YOU feel safe in your house, right? What precautions have you physically put into place to protect you from the outside?

Let's START with this!

Grandma has the BEST cookie recipe on planet earth! Everyone likes Grandma's cookies! Everyone want's Grandma's cookies!

YOU want those cookies! YOU just gotta have those cookies! YOUR mouth is watering for those cookies!

You know nothing about Grandma's house. YOU have never been in there for 20 years!

## Defensive Provisions

What defensive provisions does Grandma have in her house to block the predators from coming in and getting her cookies?

- Does she have a door or doors?
- Does she have locks on those doors?
- Does she have windows?
- Does she have an alarm?
- Does she have a dog?
- Does she live alone?
- YOU take it for granted she has electric and water, you know utilities.
- If she has electric? What defensive measures require electric? Maybe she has an alarm?
- If she has an alarm, does that alarm have a battery back-up in case the electric goes out?
- What kind of alarm does she have, if she has one? Does it have window sensors, glass break sensors, movement detectors, infra-red, etc.?

How do you know? How do you find out?

RESEARCH! INVESTIGATE!

A hacker might wake up one morning and decide to hack something or someone for some reason, but if he/she wants to stay out of jail, they DO THEIR RESEARCH!

ALL it takes in ONE slip-up or mistake at the wrong time to go to jail!

Grandma KNOWS everyone LIKES her cookies! Grandma KNOWS somebody MIGHT want to steal her cookies! Grandma has a recipe for those cookies! Where does Grandma keep the recipe for her cookies? Has anyone ever done a story about Grandma and her cookies? Reporters, newspaper, talk show, etc.

If so, maybe there is information she or they provide during that conversation you can use in your RESEARCH? What was said? What did she or someone else tell? Maybe unknowingly someone divulged information?

RESEARCH! HALF the battle is the Research!

# Research

Information is everywhere. In the internet world it is unlimited.

So far we know we like Grandma's cookies. We know Grandma knows we like her cookies. We know Grandma has a cookie recipe. We would take it for granted she wants to keep her recipe safe, right?

How is Grandma keeping her cookies and recipe safe?

People GENERALLY are basically all the same, in theory anyway. People get tired. People get lazy. People sometimes tell things. Sometimes they have a BIG mouth. Many times they think they are safer than they are! Many times they think they and their items are safe enough.

Think about yourself! Are you safe enough? At home, in the car, etc.?

YOU are NO different than the majority of the population!

YOU probably won't realize how vulnerable YOU are until it is too late! This is generally the norm!

The parent let's their kid play in the street! She does NOT think a thing about it! UNTIL the kid gets ran over, and it is too late! Then it is the DRIVER of the vehicles fault! Right? When you think about it: The vehicle and driver had the right to be in the road. That is where vehicles belong. Kids do not belong in the street, right?

Back to our story…

We are talking about a small time scenario. If you think of a LARGE corporation, they are always in the news spouting off about how big they are, and how safe they are, and how they have the most current protections. Always boasting and bragging. If you dig a little you might be surprised what you find in your research.
It does not really matter how small or large the proposed victim is, the procedure and steps are the same.

- Who is the victim?
- What is the victim?
- What is the prize?
- What is the risk?
- Risk compared to Prize?

## R i s k

Now you have done your research. Through that research you may have, and probably have come up with even more questions. Questions that need an answer! YOU can NEVER do TOO much research! YOU can never be TOO careful! Prison and jail is NOT a place YOU want to be!

Part of the risk isn't just the obstacles you are trying to overcome.

Has something been put into place to track YOU or watch YOU when you are trying to breach something, a perimeter or network?

If you are walking past Grandma's house do lights come on outside? Are their cameras outside? Can you see them? Maybe you cannot see something that is there? Is it worth the risk?

If you are trying to get Grandma's cookie recipe, where is it? IS it in a computer, a laptop, a server, a database, etc.? Where is it? Who setup the location where the recipe is stored? Was it a layman or a professional? Is there someone hired 24/7 to physically watch monitors and screens to track and watch someone moving around the perimeter of Grandma's house? Or not? If the recipe is on a network, is there someone there watching and tracking network movement and traffic 24/7 in and out of that network? Do you know?

A lot of questions, right?

Welcome to the world of the Offensive!

# 2 ... FIRST THINGS FIRST

I don't know how many times I have seen advertisements on TV about a post-secondary educational facility offering degrees, certificates, and coursework. I don't know how many times I have seen advertisements for educational facilities offering 100% online degrees, certificates, and coursework. Why do I mention this? For YOU to understand what YOU may be getting into.

## Learning by Design

I have mentioned before in my courses. I have talked about the five senses of learning. These are the senses of hearing, smelling, tasting, feeling, and speaking. We would all agree that the five senses make up the human element and how that human element relates, expresses, and reacts to learning. It seems simple when you think about it. My question is: If the goal was to reach 100% of the learning ability of the student, and each of the five senses is comprised of 20% of that learning ability, how can we teach in a way that collaborates with all the five senses to have a higher level of learning?

During one of my master's degrees, I wrote a paper on the five senses of learning. I mentioned it to one of my professors at that time, and he said I should look at researching the topic further as it was a topic brought out at meetings and seminars then, and until then, there were no answers, just questions. We all know how life leads us in other directions than those proposed. This has been a topic in my mind for many years; hence, it is the reason for bringing it up here and a few of my other writings. I have had many doctoral credit hours in instructional technology, distance education, and curriculum development, and I often wonder how successful online coursework can be.

In my opinion, anything can be taught. Anything can be physically on campus. Anything can be taught online. Hence lies the question: What and how do you as an educator make that happen for the students to receive the highest percentage of learning possible? What must you do in your classroom to get the highest percentage of your points across? If each of the five senses needs to be *energized* or *excited*, how does the educator make this connection for the student? In a typical physical classroom or laboratory, you can reach 20% in reading (eyes), 20% in listening (ears), 20% in touching (hands), and 20% in speaking if the participants collaborate together, for a total of 80%, right?

So, here we are and why we are having this course as a physical on-campus course. To get the maximum learning experience possible. You cannot take the significance of hands-on learning for granted. Learning is through touching and feeling with the hands. I hear this from many students; *I am a hands-on learner.* Some students know of that concept and comprehend how best they learn. Some have even mentioned the concept of right-brain and left-brain and can briefly explain. Sometimes, I have students who explain to me the concept of multitasking and why it is not possible with the wiring of the human brain. It is boggling that some students are on the same path as me, and it has taken me quite a few years to get where I am through all the research I have done. I guess we can attribute that to Generation Z.

One thing that helped me as a student was physically writing what I wanted to remember. You do not see that much today, as everything we want as educators is provided digitally. It might be nice to step back in time and get assignments physically written, scanned, and sent to us. That could help students in that sense. Just a thought.

This is not to say that some career areas or fields cannot be taught 100% online; they can. Many instructional methods and learning methods directly relate to the student's age, motivation, grade level, and whether the student is currently in their chosen career field or trying to get into the career field after graduation. My point is that anything can be taught in any mode; which is the best mode for the students to get the best education and career chance someone is paying?

If students are not getting the highest educational value, they have a higher chance of lowering retention rates. Are these retention rates not applicable to post-graduation? We, as educators, want our students to be career-successful. We want our students to tell other potential students of their successes and send them to our educational institutions. If the administration is only worried about the data and statistical side of their institutions, would these post-graduation students not also be of interest to them?

There is another theory related to the five senses and it is called the universal design for learning, put together by proponents of online education. They propose what they call networks: Recognition, Strategic, and Affective Networks. They say the Recognition Network is the 'what' of learning and it is how we gather facts and categorize what we see, hear, and read. They say the Strategic Network is the 'how' of learning and it is how we plan and perform tasks and organize and express our ideas. Lastly, they say the Affective Network is the 'why' of leaning and it is how learners get engaged and stay motivated, and how they are challenged, excited and or interested. It is really another way to look at the five senses. It is kind of like twisting something around to meet your needs. It makes sense to some as does the other concept. It depends upon what side you are on.

## Campus or Online

I remember when correspondence schools were abundant and advertising. Correspondence schools were predominantly for non-traditional students. They were mainly for older people, who were already employed in their relative fields, to learn more of their craft, and possibly gain a higher position or more responsibility at their perspective companies. They were not designed nor developed for the typical undergraduate student. Correspondence school educations were all carried out through the US mail service. They send YOU materials to study, YOU return assignments, YOU get graded, and then YOU finish. Similar to an asynchronous online education.

Prevalent today is the online education, the sequel to the correspondence school. The online educational facility generally offers synchronous or asynchronous forms of coursework. In synchronous coursework you meet online as a team to discuss and learn, and in asynchronous you have no set meeting times with other classmates, you are pretty much on-your-own.

There are more questions here than just: Am I comfortable basically teaching and learning myself at my own pace or do I need the motivation and drive of peers and professors within a campus environ?

## A c c r e d i t a t i o n s

I am not sure that just any human entity or entities can pop up with the bright idea that they want to open an educational facility, but maybe they can, all it takes is money? Anyone can offer a fancy paid advertisement. What YOU must look at are accreditations. All educational facilities can be reviewed by the Department of Education website. If YOU are interested they are easy to find. Now, that isn't to say that all coursework offered has to have accreditations, but YOU need to understand when accreditations need to be sought out and when they do not. Don't take it for granted that a flashy advertisement will be completely honest with YOU. Advertisements cost money and are made to make money from consumers, YOU.

## Will Anyone Hire Me?

Does the educational facility YOU are looking at have an arrangement with industry? Is industry involved in reviewing the curriculum of the educational facility YOU are thinking of applying to? This even applies to campus degrees and certifications, but most certainly applies to online educational situations.

I have recently been involved in researching data as it pertains to newly proposed degree programs and certificates using current data marketing consultants. One of the questions I have had for years has been related to degree programs, graduates of those degree programs, and the current career placement of those retained graduates.

It has become somewhat alarming to me that the only tracking educational facilities do is the tracking through alumni associations which tells the job status of members. The job status is that the students has received a job but there is no delineation as to whether that job is related to their degree or educational pathway. All we know is that they have a job after graduation. Government does mandatorily make education facilities turn in student related documentation for certain tracking but there is no delineation of career titles or job titles. All we know is that the graduated student has a job.

My question for YOU is: Regardless of the online or campus degree work, does that facility have a relationship with industry which may assist YOU in getting a job after graduation in your area of expertise?

Isn't the reason for someone paying for YOUR education is to give YOU a boost over the person who does not have the education?

# 3 ... 'THINKING HATS'

In this chapter I am going to talk about thinking. Many years ago the thinking was right-brain and left-brain. It was though that human elements had one or the other as dominant. You were either a creative or critical thinker, not 100% but more of one than the other. It sounds logical, right? Some of us are better at being creative and some of us are hard and deep thinkers, right? Then some of us think we are just the "cat's meow" at everything. My question would be: What does everyone else think about that?

I like to think of creative and critical thinking as working together. Kind of like a "Yin and Yang". Both things make you complete. I like to think of them as two brothers working together to solve a common goal. Then we have this thinking method called strategic thinking. Strategic thinking is like the cousin of two brothers. You know the third wheel when you get together, the guy who can't make a decision without looking at both sides of all issues, you know the politically correct thinker that "beats the dead horse" so-to-speak. You don't mind him being around or coming to the party, you just want him to get to the point!

*Thinking* is a series of processes we do not realize, as happening every second of every minute of every day. Pulses bouncing from left to right and right to left in our every waking moment as well as when we are at rest. Some thoughts we control, or try to control, and some thoughts we may not even recognize are being processed through our subconscious, while sleeping.

The human mind is always trying to *work things out*, to *decipher*, to *interpret*, and to *untangle* pieces of data the physical senses bring to its attention: sight, smell, hearing, taste, and touch. The senses open up a door of awareness to our minds. Once the door is opened our mind starts to analyse and process what just happened, and we usually don't even realize it is happening, it happens sometimes in the background. This is the *blank slate* each human is born with that starts to compile information form the first day it is brought into the light and continues until the final day when that light has extinguished.

During the lifecycle of this *blank slate*, foreseen and unforeseen issues and problems abound over the years. Issues that can be small or large, and simple or complex. Issues that are either under our control and or not of our making but that require our input, for a solution. When a problem or issue is sensed the brain starts to go through analysing and processing the received data.

A solution for this sensed problem or issue is limited by the current knowledge base of the recipient, and in fact each human entity is a product of its environment and we all have limitations of previous experiences and familiarities to help with our resolve.

There are two sides to the human brain, the left and the right. Both sides work together sending pulses back and forth. Some people are left-brain dominant, some are right-brain dominant and some use both-sides somewhat equally, which is a lesser percentage than the left and right dominant. People who are labelled as left-brain thinkers are said to be logically and analytically dominant. People who are labelled as right-brain thinkers are said to be innovatively and creatively dominant.

I think you get the point, enough about that, let's move on. The proceeding pages are relative to the left-brain dominant, logical *critical* thinker and the right-brain dominant, innovative *creative* thinker and the thinker that combines the two, the strategic thinker, maybe even doing this unknowingly. Problems and issues, are sensed and analysed by the brain where it decides what tools are needed to help resolve the situation. Remember now, each human has a limited knowledge base, limited by the experiences of what they have learned and acquired from each of their respective environments. Sometimes we need to use our logical side for resolve and sometimes we need use our creative side. Some of us are better at some things and others other things. Sometimes we need to think logically for a solution and sometimes we need to look at being creative.

## 'Ten Gallon' the Critical Thinker

Why the Ten Gallon Hat in relation to Critical Thinking? The Ten Gallon Hat is deep, and critical thinking is often thought of as deep or profound thinking. We'll call the Ten Gallon Hat the Thinking Hat, the Critical Thinking Hat. When I think of critical thinking, I think of logic or thinking logically. That may be a stretch to others in the field, but that is how I see it. I see it as looking at an issue or problem and realistically looking for answers to solve it, as your brain scans through the folders of knowledge you have attained throughout your short existence to find a solution. What process does the human mind need to go through to solve that issue or problem? Is it a small process with only a few steps, or is it a larger problem that requires many steps and/or sub-steps within the steps? This is what I derive as the Ten Gallon Critical Thinking Hat

As with the critical thinker, there are many ways to articulate the concept of their thinking, critically that is. Yet every substantive conception of critical thinking must contain certain core elements. Consider the following brief conceptualizations.

"Critical thinking is the intellectually disciplined process of actively and skillfully conceptualizing, applying, analyzing, synthesizing, and/or evaluating information gathered from, or generated by, observation, experience, reflection, reasoning, or communication, as a guide to belief and action. In its exemplary form, it is based on universal intellectual values that transcend subject matter divisions: clarity, accuracy, precision, consistency, relevance, sound evidence, good reasons, depth, breadth, and fairness..."

"Critical thinking is self-guided, self-disciplined thinking which attempts to reason at the highest level of quality in a fair-minded way. People who think critically consistently attempt to live rationally, reasonably and empathically. They are keenly aware of the inherently flawed nature of human thinking when left unchecked. They strive to diminish the power of their egocentric and socio-centric tendencies. They use the intellectual tools that critical thinking offers – concepts and principles that enable them to analyze, assess, and improve thinking. They work diligently to develop the intellectual virtues of intellectual integrity, intellectual humility, intellectual civility, intellectual empathy, intellectual sense of justice and confidence in reason. They realize that no matter how skilled they are as thinkers, they can always improve their reasoning abilities and they will at times fall prey to mistakes in reasoning, human irrationality, prejudices, biases, distortions, uncritically accepted social rules and taboos, self-interest, and a vested interest."

"Critical thinkers strive to improve the world in whatever ways they can and contribute to a more rational, civilized society. At the same time, they recognize the complexities often inherent in doing so. They strive never to think simplistically about complicated issues and always to consider the rights and needs of relevant others. They recognize the complexities in developing as thinkers, and commit themselves to life-long practice toward self-improvement. They embody the Socratic principle: *The unexamined life is not worth living*, because they realize that many unexamined lives together result in an uncritical, unjust, dangerous world."

Within the industrial working environment, this can be as simple as working on an assembly line and putting nut 'A' onto bolt 'B'. How many steps do you need to draw or spell out to do that simple job or task? Can just anyone or everyone do that simple task? Does everyone need the same number of steps to complete that task? Does the human mind work in all matters the same for everyone? Think about it. Do you think the same way that everyone else around you does? That is doubtful, as if you know anything about the human mind, you know that everyone is different. If all the writings throughout time are right, then each human entity or in relation to the title of this reading, the college freshman, is a product of their environment and surroundings. If correct, these are not the same for everyone. Every potential student is different.

Then there comes the additional factor of age: the age of the college freshman. If we look at statistics in relation to the college freshman, the majority of that population have just graduated high school or have graduated a few years earlier, generally a population between the ages of eighteen to twenty-two. The older we are and the more time we have spent breathing and accessing the realizations throughout our lives, the more blocks of knowledge we have acquired and retained. Our minds retain those ideas, concepts, and solutions, whether we realize it or not. From birth, the human mind is like a sponge soaking up every bit of knowledge your physical senses pick up. Some human senses are stronger and keener than others. After all, we are all different in our makeup, Right? A newborn child has often been spoken of as a *clean slate*: a *clean slate* that progressively soaks up everything it hears, sees, and feels, leading through the years to what we are as we grow older.

Let's look at a more intensive/extensive example of necessary steps to achieve a solution. What if you are thinking of an education and the educational pathway is something within the realm or area of computer science and/or information technology? I choose these realms as these are what I have been involved in throughout my existence on this planet. What issues or problems might a computer science or information technology student run into during their pathway to educational success in the classroom?

Let's first look at computer science. First off, computer science is one of the most difficult post-secondary educational programs that exist today; it is likened to engineering and the sciences. This is not to say they are the only difficult educational pathways; these are the ones I am familiar with and have knowledge of. This is not to deter you, but rather to prepare you. The career positions tied to these programs of study can be highly lucrative and pay very well. That is generally why a lot of potential students seek out these programs. If we are seeking out these programs, we need to understand what is required to be successful in them. After all, we all want to be successful, right? The purpose of getting an education is to graduate and get a good career, right? And of course, make good money, right? Why not reap the benefits that come with it, right?

Within computer science, there are a lot of programming courses, and some are statistics-related. These courses generally take more preparation and mindful thinking to process. to process and successfully work through the problems you may be given in your coursework to find correct and efficient solutions. These problems will not be as simple to solve as the nut 'A' on bolt 'B' example mentioned earlier. These will be more complex with multiple steps and sub-steps. Pages of programming languages and code to work through, to troubleshoot, and to develop.

How about information technology? When you think of information technology, you think of computers, hardware and software for computers, the networking of computers, and the security of all these things. There is a lot of memorization of the concepts and ideas within this coursework, as well as steps and sub-steps of troubleshooting devices and the planning and design of computing networks. Additionally, you will also be involved in programming related to computers and networked devices as well as website languages. These can be somewhat complicated, but they are all guided by the student and their desire to achieve and succeed. The object is not to dissuade you from seeking these programs but to inform and prepare you. You will surely come to use your Ten Gallon Hat. It will become your second nature.

## 'Sombrero' the Creative Thinker

Why the Sombrero in relation to Creative Thinking? The Sombrero has a wide brim: a wide brim that covers the possible vastness of thinking *outside the box*. Inside the box, *thinking* has the limit of the internal size of the box: the diameter, the circumference, and dimensions of the box.

We'll call the Sombrero the Creative Thinking Hat. Some of us are more 'creative' than others. Some of us are better artists than others. Some of us design, draw, paint, and illustrate, and some of us just don't seem to have that talent. Can you acquire that talent, or is it something you are either 'born with' or not? Well, in previous wording, we mentioned that human entities and authors throughout time have said babies are thought to be born with a *clean slate*, right? That is what has been said. If that is true, then that 'baby' must be trainable or teachable in some form or fashion, right? If the human entities of the world are correct, then it must be.

You just have to come into those situations where your mind needs to view what it sees in a different manner.

Looking at an issue or problem through a different *lens* than you normally see. Have you ever heard someone say "they are looking at that with rose-colored glasses?" What does that mean? That means that you are looking at something with bias. That means you are looking at something without an open mind; you are only seeing what you want to see. You are not looking past your own knowledge base. You are only trying to solve that issue with the knowledge you have attained so far through your life and not looking past that, as you may not know everything and there may be more knowledge you can attain past the point of today, at any given moment in time. Does that make sense?

The creative thinker continually digs deep into oneself and generates more, newer, better, faster, cheaper, different ideas that can be used to improve the important parts of their life, i.e. the successful manager. The creative thinker is comprised of seven distinct qualities:

1. I am curious to a fault
2. I practice zero-based thinking
3. I am willing to change
4. I am goal focused
5. I am willing to admit when I am wrong
6. I do not know everything
7. My ego will not be bruised if and when I am proven wrong

The first quality of creative thinkers is that they are curious to a fault. They are always asking questions. They never stop asking questions, and would like to find others similar to themselves. They ask questions like "Why or Why not, why can't we do that, if it hasn't been done, can we do it now?" There onslaught of questioning would be similar to that of a child, but they know why they ask, they have reasons, other than the bantering of a child.

The second quality of creative thinkers is that they practice "Zero-Based Thinking" throughout their daily routines. They continually ask themselves, "If I were not now doing what I am doing, knowing what I now know, would I start?" If their answer is no, they stop that train of curiosity , then move on to another thought project and start their questioning all over again. They say that hindsight is always 20-20. Creative thinkers move forward and do not dwell on the "what if" scenario. So many humans persist on questioning and spending vast amounts of energy on projects that when they look behind they would have never started to begin with, and generally wish they had not, then they wonder why they make so little progress and it seems to take forever.

The third quality of creative thinkers is that they are always willing to change, they are open to new suggestions and have an open mindset. They prefer to be in charge of their lives rather than being caught up in a flash flood of change that may often be inevitable and or unavoidable. The words of the truly flexible person, the person who is willing to change are simply, "I changed my mind." According to researchers, fully 70% of the decisions you make turn out to be wrong in the long run. This means that you must be willing to change your mind and try something else the majority of the time. Mental flexibility is the most important quality that you will need for success in this the 21st century.

The fourth quality of creative thinkers is their willingness to admit when they are wrong. They do not hold fast to their opinions when they are proven wrong. Researchers say that 80% of people burn up most of their mental and emotional energy defending against admitting that they made a wrong decision. True creative people are open minded, fluid, flexible and willing to both change their mind and admit that they are wrong when their earlier decisions turn out to be incorrect.

The fifth quality is that creative people can say, "I don't know." They recognize that it is impossible for anyone to know anything about everything, and it is very likely that almost everyone is wrong to some extent, no matter what they are doing. So when someone asks them a particular question that they don't know the answer so they admit it early and often. They simply say, "I don't know." And if necessary they go about finding the answer. Here's an important point. No matter what problems you have, there is someone somewhere who has had the same problem and who has already solved the problem and is using the solution today. One of the smartest and most creative things you can do is to find someone else, somewhere, who is already implementing the solution successfully and then copy him or her. The smartest person is not necessarily the person who comes up with the idea, but the one who accentuates or successfully builds upon it.

The sixth quality of creative people is that they are intensely goal focused. They know exactly what they want. They have it written down very clearly. They visualize it on a regular basis. They imagine what their goal would look like if it were a reality today. And the more they visualize and imagine their goal as a reality, the more creative they become and the faster they move toward achieving it.

The seventh quality of highly creative thinkers is that they have less ego involvement in being right. You will not bruise or crush their ego if you prove them wrong. They are always looking for and willing to accept the correct answer even if it down not come from them. They are more concerned with what is right rather than who is right. They are willing to accept ideas from any source to achieve a goal, overcome an obstacle, or solve a problem.

The most important part of creative thinking is the ability to generate ideas. And the greater the quantity of ideas that you generate, the greater the quality your ideas will be. Similar to that of a brain trust: a gathering of multiple brains coming up with multiple ideas to successfully come up with a solution. The more ideas you have, the more likely you are to have the right idea at the right time. But generating ideas is only 1% of the equation. As Thomas Edison once wrote, "Genius is one percent inspiration and 99 percent perspiration."

Your ability to come up with an idea, to test it and validate it, and then to implement it through creative thinking and execute it in your life to achieve results is the true mark of a successful IT manager. Every single time you originate a new idea, write it down, make a plan for its implementation through creative thinking and then take action, you are behaving like a genius. And the more you manage your creativity in this way, the smarter you will become. And the smarter you will become, the more you will achieve in every area of your life.

It is a rather drawn-out and lengthy concept. Basically, it means not to let the limits of what you have learned *soaked up* so far in life deter you from being able to *soak up* new things. After all, none of us know everything; we are only human entities and we are always learning, even when we grow older, we never stop learning. You may think you have stopped learning, but remember in previous paragraphs we talked about the human mind as *soaking up* as it goes along. Well, until we pass through this life, the thought is that we always gather information whether we realize it or not.

Enough explanation and background, let's get to the title at hand: Creative Thinking. Looking at what we need to do and the steps we may need to make to solve an issue or problem creatively. Could we call this thinking 'outside the box'? What does that mean? That means to find a way to solve the issue or problem at hand by using something other than the normal process and by using some mental tool or reasoning each of us may have attained throughout our lives, each one of us separately. Remember, when we talked earlier about the knowledge each of us attains throughout our daily lives and the environments we each are involved in? Remember that? That is what we are talking about. Since we all are a product of our environments since birth, maybe you have come into contact with something to help you personally solve the issue, problem, or task given. Then again, maybe not. Maybe you have not been privy to such an environment and have been somewhat sheltered or are quite young and have not experienced such situations in your limited past?

If I look at this through faculty eyes, we are often given the task of creatively finding a way to reach students. Past history shows educators that the more *senses* we can reach within a student, the more apt we are to give them an understanding of the material we are trying to convey. This brings to mind an example from my past when I was in an Associate Degree program in Computer Electronics. In one of the courses, we each bought a kit. A kit is a lot of pieces of electronic and electrical parts. These combined parts were an AC to DC voltage regulator power supply. We each bought a kit, and the object was to follow the directions and solder up and wire the kit. This kit would be used as our personal equipment in our future higher-level electronic courses. The day came when we were to plug in our power supplies for the first time to see our new inventions light up and get a passing grade.

Before I get to the *punch line*, I will give a little explanation. I transferred to this college from a Flight school in the south. At that Flight school, I was in a highly disciplined environment. At that college, I was one of the top students in my class and was often prodded by my instructors. All the instructors were ex-military, and all students towed the line. Since my father was a drill instructor in the Air Force, and that is how I grew up, I knew my place and my responsibilities. Well, if I wasn't in class at 7:00 am in the morning, the instructor would come beat on my dorm door until I answered. To make a long story short, this instructor made sure I was the best I could be.

The best I could be was to make mostly B's and some A grades for courses. My coursework was beaten into my head at that facility, and when I transferred to another college up north, I made all 'A' letter grades on everything! And I mean everything! Thanks to my previous instructors and their pushing me to be my best! At my new college, I was quickly made the course mentor and assistant for all my electronic/electric courses. I was the kid that helped the struggling students.

Back to the story and the punchline. I plugged my power supply in and passed the class without a hitch. My best friend plugged hers in and BANG! Smoke filled the room! It was like an old Batman serial rerun! Bang! Boom! Pow! But with the addition of a lot of smoke! And the smell was horrible! Have you ever smelled burning electronics? Well, needless to say, it wasn't pleasant, and it does have a smell all its own. Well, nobody got hurt as each power supply was in a metal case with knobs and leads. A good thing, right?

My friend was heartbroken. Something within her power supply exploded. She opened the case, cleared the smoke, and looked to see what had gone wrong. She could not find the problem as she looked through the *rose-colored glasses* we mentioned above. She could see the problem as she was looking at the issue with the bias that she had done everything correctly as per the instructions. She pushed it over to me and asked if I would take a look. In less than a minute, I saw the problem. I pushed it back to her and told her to really look! I asked her a few questions.

One was: Throughout ALL the classes we have had in this program talking about electrical and electronic devices, are there any of them that are directional? Meaning they can only go one way! She looked again. Aha, she was able to see it now, she put the capacitor in backward! In a capacitor, one lead is positive and one lead is negative. If you put it in backward, it will explode! Well, it exploded! Luckily it was inside a metal case as it was a rather large capacitor.

What does this story have to do with creative thinking? If I were the instructor of an electronic course and I purposely had students solder in a capacitor in the wrong direction, then the student energized the device. Trust me: That student would always remember the BANG and the burnt electronic smell for the rest of their life where they would not let it happen again. Would this not be a creative way of thinking to get a concept or idea into the mind of a student? I rest my case.

Through all my years of being in management and supervisory positions, giving presentations, and being the previous owner of an IT corporation, I have seen ideas from many authors discussing and laying out what they think are traits of managers and supervisors. In addition to being a manager or supervisor, which is a leader in many aspects, they also need to add traits of a follower as they are not the top tier of the corporate structure; everyone has a boss, right? Below I will propose what I think to be additional hats relative to leaders and followers, which I feel run parallel to the college freshman for their goal in achieving more than simple success and passing, but for attaining above-and-beyond success. The success that needs to be achieved by the graduating senior in their attempt to compete in the marketplace with all the other graduates around the world. The layout I propose is to provide individuals a planned method to *think* cohesively to be more effective in attaining results. What does that mean?

The foundation of this layout is that the human brain goes through a number of instructions or steps, if you will, to develop a plan of attack to solve a problem.

Each instruction or step is required and is a necessity to solve the problem or task successfully. The thought is that each instruction or step when activated will unconsciously bring forth certain aspects of thought for the other instruction or step to be triggered, therefore coming up with a viable solution.

I will say this. These *instructions or steps* are not ways of thinking that all college freshmen share or may even possess, but I do think, however, that these *instructions or steps* can be a learned trait. These instructions or steps can be attained through educational reinforcement and practice. Growing up, didn't we always hear *Practice makes perfect*? Well, here we are, practice does make perfect, at least we are told. The more you practice, the better you get at it, right? Is it not easier to review work that you know has been successfully completed, as in a template, than it is to start from scratch with no provision of an example? It is like asking someone to reinvent the wheel when you have access to a perfectly good example of a wheel, right? What is the point?

Do we need an example here? Okay, let me set the stage. The first post-secondary school I went to for a degree was a Flight college in the south. I was an Avionics major, and my roommate was a Flight major. My roommate had some experience in flying and he wanted to get more flight time and a degree. He was very particular about his aircraft and didn't leave many things to chance when he flew. It seemed as though he was always flying when other students were just kind of hanging out. One of the things he liked was that one of the flight instructors had a similar background as he had, and he also wanted to get a lot of flight time, so they generally scheduled their flights together, instructor and student.

In the realm of flight, there are two ratings pilots achieve: VFR and IFR. VFR is Visual Flight Rating, and IFR is Instrument Flight Rating. Both of these ratings deal with eyesight. Visual is what you see inside and outside the cockpit and how you deal with what you actually see visually and how you react and deal with it. Instrument is where you ONLY use the instruments to see and project what to do next in a flight situation. Make sense? So, my roommate had achieved both of these ratings. Remember, I said my roommate had spent a lot of time with one certain instructor during his time at the college. SO, on to my story.

I came back to the dorm one night, all the lights were out, and my roommate was sitting on the edge of his bed, very quiet. This was unlike him, so I knew something had happened that may be life-changing. Four hours ago, my roommate was up with a different instructor getting some extra flight time. He had to choose this other instructor as the one he usually scheduled with was up in the air with another student. My roommate and his new instructor are up in one airplane, and his usual instructor and another student are up in another. I don't remember what class-level storm came up, but it was rough, and both airplanes were caught in the storm. For over three hours, both of these airplanes were buzzing around the sky. Lightning struck my roommate's airplane, taking out all the internal and external lights. The only light still on were the instrument lights. The cockpit was dark, and you could not even see the one person sitting next to you.

The only time you could see something outside the windows was when the lightning flashed. The radio was damaged also, and every now and then, you could hear garbled talk from the other airplane and the flight base towers: In and out, in and out, bits and pieces of conversations. All my roommate could really hear was someone talking about 1000 feet. He didn't know whether it meant his aircraft was to go to 1000 feet or if the other airplane was to be at 1000 feet. He could not make out the whole conversation. The new instructor with my roommate was not at all comfortable with the situation, so my roommate took charge. Like I said, my roommate was a particular guy and had no problem taking over. He was confident in his training. If anyone knows anything about an airplane pilot, they are cocky and confident!

After several hours of struggle, it is pitch black outside, and lightning is flashing. My roommate hears an airplane engine, and it is close by. The lightning flashes, and right in front of my roommate's airplane is the other plane directly in front of him at the same altitude. My roommate said his whole life flashed before his eyes, and during the brief lightning strike, he could see the eyes of the others in the other airplane. He didn't hesitate, pulled up on the yoke, and he said it was like his aircraft was standing still, without motion. In that brief instant, it was over! All four were safe! The instructor of the other airplane pushed his yoke down.

The two students and instructors are alive today because my roommate was in charge of one airplane, and his usual instructor was in charge of the other. Those two had trained together many, many times for such a scenario as this.

My roommate is a highly successful pilot for a major airline today, and we talk all the time. Practice made this perfect.

How about another quick example, a little different? I tell you to run a race. I give you the starting point and the ending point, but I leave out any specifics or limitations of the race. Then YOUR mind begins to start sorting, calculating, and planning. Do I have enough information? Do I need to start at a certain time? Do I need to get to the endpoint at a certain time? What mode of transportation am I to use? How many other questions would or could a participant ask? We already can see how creativity ties in with the success of a student from the information previously presented. Creativity or Creative Thinking being one of the two main necessities mentioned in detail above along with Critical Thinking.

## 'Boonie' the Strategic Thinker

Why the Boonie in relation to Strategic Thinking? The Boonie hat or cap has a wide flexible brim that protects the wearer from harsh surrounding elements. Typically, you see the

Boonie work by trained military personnel, personnel sent to carry out life or death missions using both creative and critical thinking. Hence, the strategic thinker uses both thinking ideologies.

The strategic thinker is split into four distinctive groups, each one which guides to the next group, to a final outcome. They are: understanding a strategy; analyzing the position; planning a strategy; and implementing the strategy.

The first section called Understanding a Strategy, speaks of the first basic components that you should consider when looking to define a strategy and the basic components involved in thinking of solutions in a strategic way. Are you as an IT manager looking for short-term results or are you looking for future results? The IT manager should look at the employees and staff involved and seek to find which is better suited to assist in the process to find a solution which will achieve success. The IT manager can take a lot of waste and lost time out of the equation if you avoid guesswork and stick with the facts and statistical data. For success in the beginning stages and even in the final stages you must always keep reviewing the process to allow you to stay on track and not lose sight of the purpose of your project.

The second section called Analyzing the Position, speaks basically of knowing the audience you are getting an answer for, knowing what influences the results, knowing your audience needs, knowing your competitors, assessing yourself and your IT employee's skill and abilities and summarizing the data analysis of all of these factors combined. Every problem has at least one influencing factor this could be anything from monetary values to professional notoriety. What exactly is required of you by the company who has hired your IT firm or is the issue in-house? What are the audience expectations and limits? What are the aspects of competitors? What skills and knowledge does your IT solution team possess? When you combine all of this information together you will be better able to come up with selecting a plan of strategy that will assist your IT business in achieving success.

The third section called Planning a Strategy, speaks of the five stages to consider when completing a strategic planning project. Define the purpose, determine the advantages, set the boundaries of the project, choose the main areas to emphasize or which stand out, and lastly estimate the amount of money and time which will be allotted for the project solution. The IT manager should make sure that everyone involved in this project and solution is on the same page so that there is no conflict in either the project team camp or the customer's camp. Toward the end of this section there are two final steps in this process, to test to validate the strategies potential success that you have compiled and to make sure that communication has been successful and informed all of the people who need to be involved in this project.

The fourth and final section called Implementing Strategy is I would say the hardest step to complete. This step involves every single person at every level. When implementing a strategy there are several steps in the beginning of implementation which are setting priorities for the change: actually planning the change;

assessing the potential risks involved in the change; and finally reviewing the targeted goals presented. Now we come to the hardest part that of motivating the staff. The majority of people I believe are scared of changes. Any internal or external movement in a corporate setting usually puts all employees on pins and needles. Usually if there is a change in the corporate situation that means that someone has a bright idea of improving something and that generally means that the improvement is going to benefit the company and not the employees.

You can bet that if the strategy benefits the shareholders that it matters not if you are a part of it or not so the only choice you have is to go along with it and hope for the best. After the motivational step there are three final steps to go through and they are monitoring the performance of the project after implementing, reviewing and analyzing the acquired data, and being flexible by looking at the data and if there are changes or alterations to be made to be successful then you must be open to suggestions and maybe even starting this process over again.

**Seven Additional Hats**

In addition to the three thinking hats there are additional hats students and graduates need to wear to continue to be successful and useful products within the workplace and society.

## White Hard of the Manager

Why the White hard hat? Have you ever been to or  seen on television a construction site? If you pay attention and look for the 'White hard' hats, the people wearing those are the managers, supervisors, and organizers of that construction project.

Who is responsible for your education? You are the one on the ground, you are the one taking courses. It does not matter if you are footing the bill or if you are on grants and or scholarships, you are the sole entity responsible for your failures or successes, for your program degree attainment or failure. You are the one. You may have guides, conductors, and advisors along the way, but in reality, you are the one responsible. You should know before enrolling in any program how many courses and or credits that program entails. You should know how many projected semesters you need to complete to successfully attain your degree.

You should know each semester which courses are offered and available. You should register and enroll in them before they fill up with students and are closed, leaving you to make changes that may extend your graduation date. At some point, there may be someone else who is assisting you that you can lay some blame on, but in reality, you are the one responsible. Take charge of your education. You may be in other courses with other students each semester, where we like to say "we are all in this together". On one hand, that is correct, but on another, you are in the kayak paddling alone up the river. Sinking or swimming is up to you. The assistance you have along your path is the life jacket, the preserver that keeps you from drowning if you fall in. These would include guides, conductors, and advisors. They are your safety net. They are the ones you ask to make sure you are doing the right things.

Relating to the topic of management. Each semester I find myself being asked if I want to teach a course virtually or physically. I have even had students ask me this same question. I will give more than a brief explanation here, but the background is relevant to see the bigger picture. Why are some courses taught virtually and some physically, and who decides this? This will take a little while for me to explain, so bear with me as this answer has several parts and will be quite long.

I have done quite a bit of research over my years related to the human brain, how it works, and how it develops. There has been a myriad of research related to the human brain, and we still know very little, but are learning new things all the time. Specialists tell us that people learn differently. The brain is the guiding light of each human, the human is the product of their environment, and then therefore the brain is the product of the human's environment.

The brain works together as a unit, but there are two sides within the brain: the *left side* and the *right side*. The *left side* is associated with language handling, methodical thinking, and logic. The *right side* is associated with creativity, general thinking, and instinct. The question is: Can a human, or is a human, left side or right side dominant? Theories abound that yes, we can be either or. That is why some people are good at some things and others are not.

Let's take algebra and trigonometry as examples. I made straight A's in college in Trigonometry and struggled in Algebra. I could draw a picture of a *trig* problem, see it work, and solve it. I couldn't draw a picture of an algebra problem, see it work, and solve it. When I was in elementary and secondary school, we had college-bound students and work-bound students. College-bound students took higher-level math courses and work-bound or vocational school-bound students took regular math or business math. I spent a lot of time with math tutors, and my best friend was a math major, and I just didn't get it, but I passed first with a 'D' then with a 'C'. To this day, I still don't see how it works. So, am I the only human on this planet that does not get Algebra and has tried? I doubt it. I believe some students just won't get it no matter how hard they try. I relate this to programming languages as well.

When you take what I just said and you add this: Some courses have topics that are easier to grasp than others. Some courses have a lot of terminology to remember, and some courses have practice. Think about an anatomy course where you have internal and external body parts. You memorize the names of each item, its location, and purpose. Liken this anatomy course to a course in Cybersecurity. There is a lot of memorization, placement, and usage, right? Well, that course might be taught just as easily virtually or physically. The instructor may be able to get the point across just as easily using either method, right?

If we look at more of an abstract course, say algebra, calculus, or a programming language, it could be more difficult to get those points across to the student. Also, it could possibly present issues for the instructor trying to get those points across to every student. Through all of the education I have had in my past, I have spoken to a lot of teachers, during elementary school, junior high, high school, and college. Back then, teachers would say they were told to teach to the majority of the class. If they could 'reach' the majority of the class, they were doing their job. The majority, to me, means 51%, right? I remember teachers trying all kinds of things in the classroom to get their points across to students, and sometimes it just didn't work. You still had the full gamut of students: A's, B's, C's, D's, and F's.

Then you have virtual course-related terms as synchronous and asynchronous. Synchronous is where the instructor meets with the whole class online and goes through their song-and-dance to the students. Asynchronous is where the instructor generally makes videos for the students in the class, as the class has no specified meeting dates and or times. The students view the videos on their own time. With asynchronous, other factors need to be implemented within the course to get and give feedback to students, as they are never in presence of the instructor, unless they schedule something and arrangements are made. Virtual synchronous is similar to the physical classroom in many aspects, other than the physicality of the participants.

Today, educators have different standards, goals, and theories for classroom instruction. In my opinion, some students, no matter how hard they try, may just not understand certain topics. Their brain may just not work that way. Why do some students in a programming class or any class, for that matter, get all A's and some get all C's? Is it the student's fault or the instructor's fault? Can the instructor spend countless hours with one student? Where does that extra time come from? Is it the mode of instruction, virtual or physical? As you can see, a lot of questions get raised. Hopefully, I have given a somewhat understandable answer to your question. The answer, in short, is: The instructor chooses the mode of instruction, depending upon if they feel their topic is best taught and grasped by the student virtually, physically, or either. Grasped and comprehended by not just the majority, 51% of students, but all of the students.

All in all, this category comes down to this: Managing your time. How many classes do you have? When do they meet? What assignments are there to complete? When are those assignments due? How do I manage my time to complete everything I need to be a success and get a passing grade? What are the penalties if I get side-tracked? It just does not seem like I have enough time in the day for all I am involved in. How do I cope?

From years of involvement within industry and education, the number one issue I have seen is the worst word you can utter or the poorest practice you could acquire: Procrastination. Putting things off until tomorrow when you can and should get them done today. Throughout my life, I have never been privy to this practice. How have I made this a priority? If you are anything like me, if you are sick you do not want to be bothered! You want to be left alone until the issue subsides. My feeling is that if I complete the task right away, in the chance that I do get sick, I will not be bothered as I have already completed the task! Makes sense to me.

One last thing here: Never get all the assignments in a course completed and the last week of class of the semester ask the professor or instructor "If I don't complete the final exam what will my grade be for this course"? That just doesn't make the student look good. It tells the professor or instructor the student only wants to do the least amount of work to pass the class. Never a good look for you, right?

## Fedora of the Conversant

Why the Fedora? The Fedora has a long history since  the 1800s. Have you ever seen the movie *Indiana Jones*? The world traveler, professor, archaeologist, and researcher. Need I say more?

This has to do with the college freshman 'being informed'. There are two sides of this category: the physical and psychological. Physical is the brick-and-mortar makeup of the campus and its maintained structures. Psychological is the information gathered and retained by the brain of the college freshman. Whenever you step on campus, you should seek out and know where everything is. You should know what buildings on campus relate to you and your studies. You should know your environment. You should know who to contact for specific questions. You are not in control of all things on a college campus, but you should know your surroundings and where things are and who is responsible for what. Know where the exit doors are. Know what to do in any given drastic or catastrophic situation.

Yes, there are generally orientation courses or meetings for newcomers, but the realization is that you are responsible. You are responsible to know what is where and how to get there. Seeking information is your responsibility.

I don't know of any educational institution that has a staff or faculty made up of people with extrasensory perception (ESP). What does that mean? That means that nobody or no one on a college campus knows what you are thinking or that you need or want to ask a question. Sometimes we may get a premonition of sorts by the look or the expression on your face and see the confusion, but all in all, we don't know you from the other students in the room. However, we do, in time, get to know certain aspects of our students after a few semesters. I remember in grade school, on the first day of class, our teachers would have us stand up in front of the class, announce who we were, and maybe say something about ourselves. At the post-secondary level, this may still be an option for some faculty, but in larger schools, this may not be a tool looked at as useful. In some courses, you may have 10, 30, or even over 100 students. The larger the student population, the more likely you are to be seen as a number instead of a name. Don't depend on the instructor or professor knowing who you are; take charge and let them know who you are by standing out from the rest. 'This is me, I am here, see me.'

Generally, faculty are more prone to *know your face* than staff, as faculty in your program will surely come into contact with you for several courses, if not a majority of them. We want to know you. We want to know what your interests are. We want to know if you are having issues. We want to know why you have stopped coming to class. We want to know why you have not turned in any assignments for three weeks. Like I mentioned before: We are not mind readers. We are just like you. We were in your shoes once, twice, or maybe even three or more times. We know what it is like to sit where you are sitting. We didn't want to be embarrassed asking what we think might be a stupid question. I have always heard "The only stupid question is the one left unasked". We as faculty know you are getting an education and that you do not have one already. This we know or pretty much expect anyway. We don't know unless you tell us.

Get to know the faculty in your major area. Let them know what your interests are. Don't wait for them to come to you; beat them to the punch. Let those faculty know you are willing and want to do more than just pass courses and graduate. Let them know you want to go the extra mile. You want your name to be on the lips of faculty when you are looking for a good internship that could possibly lead to a career job position. Let them know you want to stick out from the other graduating students each semester from around the world. These are the students you are competing with for career positions. You have to stick out from all those graduates. There is much more than just getting an 'A' in your courses. Ask job recruiters and they will tell you they want more than just a high GPA. How many college graduates are there each semester? Do some research in your field and see? You are competing with all those other graduating seniors. How many graduate college each semester? How many are you competing with? Do some research?

In relation to graduating seniors, currently in the United States, there are 600,000 computer science and information technology jobs available, today. Why have they not been filled? Why do they stay listed and not filled and closed? That is another related answer and another reason for the graduating student to stick out from the rest. These are highly skilled positions. These are not just your typical retail department store jobs, but are detailed positions with employers seeking their idea of what they are looking for in an employee. They will not just accept and hire based on the fact that you hold a degree. What does holding a degree mean? It means you went through a certain amount of courses, you retained enough information to pass those courses, and you completed a degree. Basically, the attainment of a degree means the holder has completed an acceptable amount of steps and is trainable. Trainable for other information if the need arises. Did I mention that computer science and engineering related coursework and programs can be some of the most challenging?

One thing I want to mention before I get into interviews is *know your subject matter*. It is easy to just go through a course and do just enough to get by and pass. You have a rude awakening coming if you think that is all you need to do to get a good job or career started. I have mentioned before go-above-and-beyond. Do more than the average expectation. If a textbook is used in the class read the chapters and comprehend the material, or at least try your best. Be prepared for the interview. This is where the potential employer gets their first look at you and what you know.

When you receive the degree, you will find yourself filling out applications and going to interviews. This is the time when you will find out if you have done all you could have in order to make yourself more viable. This is when they look at your resume and see that you only completed a degree program or if you were one of the top graduates who not only completed a degree program but was also involved in other educational or extracurricular activities as well. If you were doing the hiring, which graduate would you rather have on your team? The one who did just enough to get by and receive a degree, or the one who not only received the degree but went above and beyond. I think we all know which one you would pick. Become involved in your education. Do more than just the minimum to graduate. Let your faculty know your intentions. If you do not know, ask!

Along with this, we have a couple of items also needing attention and thought: Attitude and Appearance or Attitude and Persona. I think persona is the word I am looking for? Let me explain a little better. Attitude has a bearing during your educational journey, and it also has a lot to deal with in relation to your attitude while speaking and talking to potential employers and employment recruiters. For example: I was on campus one day, and I went to a department where a student was working as a work-study. By the end of the semester, she was going to graduate. I knew her rather well as she was a student of mine. She began by telling me she had not learned anything during her educational journey, she had no idea what job she could get after graduation, and she just didn't know what she was going to do.

Wow, I thought, how low of an opinion of herself she must have, after all, she passed with a decent GPA and she was pretty good about attending classes, so then what was her issue? I did a little talking around, and it turns out her boyfriend, by whom she had two kids, was in jail. She lived at home with her single mother, and she had not even applied for any employment positions. I spoke with her a few days later, and she had never put together a resume and was not a member of any job-related online message boards or communities. As an answer to her plight, apparently she had gone to no lengths or trouble to seek employment or even put together anything to promote herself.

Well, whose fault is it if you take no initiative? Like I had mentioned before, there is not going to be a knock on your door; you have to do the knocking. For someone who spent almost five years to get a BS degree, she really should have had some pep talks during those years. The point here is to have a positive attitude, go the extra mile, do your best, and you will succeed. When in the employment realm, these are people just like you and me; they put on their clothes the same way, they have the same problems, doubts, and whatever else you can think of. The one thing they have different from you is they are on the other side of the fence doing the hiring, looking at you! Yes, looking at you! Why do you think they want to personally sit down and meet with you or want to meet with you virtually? Because they want to see your face, your expressions when they ask you questions, and the way you carry yourself. They want to see your positivity, they want to see that you know what you are talking about, and they want to see if you will fit into their idea of what an employee needs to be within their company.

Yes, they want to see your attitude and personality, and they want to see if you have the tools to do the job you are trying to get from them. Oh no, there is something added here I called tools. Yes, tools. How about an example: Right after high school I didn't really know what I wanted to do, but I had always been good with my hands. I had been involved in construction as a ditch digger, hod carrier, bricklayer, carpenter, painter – you know, all the skills. Dad always said if you don't like one job, try something else until you find one you like, so I knew how to do that. I tried a lot of things. I was good at all of those skills, and for some reason I don't remember, I got involved with a large painting contractor – a high-quality painting contractor. Anyway, I worked there for a year or so and decided to move back to my home state as I had a girlfriend there, and we had been proposing to get married. All boys and men know how that is – that is the only girl on the whole planet, and she is the one for us, and it is meant to last forever, right?

Well, I gave my two-week notice, and my boss, the owner of the company, pleaded with me to stay. I was offered my own crew and a brand new Chevrolet IROC Z-28 if I would stay! It was the first year of the International Race of Champions model (IROC), and I could also pick the color. We all know how this story turned out, don't we? I turned his offer down and left anyway. When I went to my new state, I easily got a job with one of the highest quality painting contractors in the Bluegrass area. All we did were high-class mansions and horse farm estates. I was very good at my job. After several months, we were working at a mansion, and the owner of our company came by and told us that later in the day, an experienced painter was coming to work with us. Later that day, a car pulled up, and a person got out.

A man in his 40s carrying a K-mart bag seemed to have just gone to K-mart. We were curious as he came up the steps. He came up the steps, opened his bag, and pulled out a six-dollar painting kit. You know, the ones for a homeowner who needs to do a little cheap touch-up painting. A plastic roller pan, a two-dollar brush, a fifty-cent roller cover, and a cheap thin drop cloth. The boss of our crew asked him how long he had been painting professionally, and the man said, "Oh, for many years". My boss asked if the tools he brought with him were the tools he always used when he painted professionally. The guy said yes, that he always used those tools, and he bought them new for every job. The man added one additional question: "Where do you want me to get started"? My boss looked at the guy and said, "Well, I don't know where to put you. All I do know is that you are not going to start here. Thanks for coming." Then the guy put the kit back in his K-mart bag and left, mad!

My point is, the supposed professional painter did not have the correct tools for the job, and a professional knew what tools were needed for the job and that the guy did not have them. In addition, when the guy said he always used new paint tools for every job, the professional knew then the guy had probably never had any real professional guidance or training by another real professional painter. A real painter isn't going to use a two or three-dollar paintbrush. I have seen and used brushes costing twenty-five to fifty dollars, and many of us painters used them for months and sometimes years. I even saw a hundred-dollar brush one time in a raffle. The point here is to possess the correct tools for the job. If you don't know what they are, ask someone who knows. If you don't have them, find out where to get them and acquire them.

Speaking of tools, these aren't just physical tools as in the story. Tools can also be internal skills. Internal tools or soft skills, as they are better known: cooperation, communication, motivation, initiative, flexibility, imagination, and quite a few others. These are often called *soft skills*. *Soft skills* are social and personable qualities employers are looking for in potential employees, in addition to the typical skills a graduating student may possess. There are too many *soft skills* to mention here, so my advice is to do some research and see which skills you possess, which skills you need to work on to strengthen, and what skills you need to acquire.

The last item in this category I want to share is appearance or maybe persona might be a better choice for a word. I have spoken about the need to become involved – involved in whatever situations you feel comfortable with, as well as the need to become involved with the professors in your major field of study. Let them know your interests, your goals, and your potential. This can be critical throughout your stay at an educational institution, not only to present your positive attitude but to show your willingness to go above and beyond and to show professors you will make a great positive example of what can come out of their college as a graduate.

This item is hard to compile to get my point across; let me give an example. Have you ever heard the expression "If it walks like a duck and quacks like a duck, it must be a duck"? My sister and I were coming back from lunch one day, and I saw a student of mine coming out of a building. I said, "Isn't that so-and-so"? And she said yes. I mentioned he must have been at a beach party as he had on shorts, a Hawaiian shirt, sunglasses, and gold chains. I had not heard of a beach party in that building today. She said, "No, I spoke to him this morning, and he had a job interview on campus with such-and-such". "Well, drop me off, and I'll see what's going on with him." I got out of the car, walked up to him, and asked how things were going. He said they were going well and he had just had an interview with such-and-such. I asked how the interview had gone, and he said it had gone just fine. I asked if he had changed clothes since his interview. He said no, that he just went as he was dressed. So, I said, "You went dressed like that, and the interview went well". He said it had. The next line out of my mouth was, "All I can say is I know such-and-such extremely well, and if you were dressed like this at the interview, for a full-time permanent position with such-and-such, then no, the interview did not go well". He looked at me and said, "Oh well, I really don't care anyway"!

For one, I was surprised at the attitude; then secondly, I was surprised at the beach attire for a graduate student seeking a professional career position. I expected more from one of my students who made all A's, completed a BS with me, and was in the final semesters of an MS degree again with me. This student always went above and beyond. If he had contacted me that morning, I would have given him advice on how to *dress for success*. My point here is: If you don't care, others don't care either. If the job does not matter to you, then why bother the interviewer as they have better things to do than waste yours and their time? Portray yourself to others as they expect you to be portrayed to them. If you are seeking a lifeguard job, dress and present yourself as a lifeguard. That is what they expect. You don't wear a three-piece suit to interview as a lifeguard, or do you? If you do, maybe you need to rethink yourself, right?

If you are unsure, ask someone who might know the answers. Always be prepared. Are you willing to do all you can to get and keep a career position? If you spend a lot of time watching television, shows on television are made and designed to get viewers to watch them. Even the so-called realism shows are put on for people to tune in. The more controversy and issues they add to the show, the more the people will view it. It isn't real, so don't take their fashion sense as advice. My real advice here is: We all, at some point in our lives, wanted to be a *rebel* or stick out so people would see us, right? That is all good and fine, but wait to show them your *rebel* side after you have been there a few years and they have become comfortable with you and realize your positive addition within their environment, right?

You might be asking, what does all this have to do with my college years? This is a lot about interviews and seeking career opportunities, right? Well, isn't the purpose for spending years getting an education to better prepare for a career position afterward? If not, what is the purpose?

One other thing: We hear all around us that college is supposed to be the best years of our lives. There is no need to dress up to be a college student. A college student should be comfortable, so wear your crocs, your sweatpants, and your pajamas to class. Nobody cares. That is part of the freedom of being a college student. The issue arises when you make your way out into the world to pursue success. Others are watching you, and those are the ones you sometimes have to please – the holders of the purse strings.

# Pith of the Explorer

Why the Pith? The Pith Helmet, better known as the Safari Helmet. Throughout history, the Pith has been used to fend off the sun and rain in many climates where wearers were carrying out searching and researching projects. Hence, the Pith of an explorer.

This category is most useful throughout the college career of the accepted freshman as well as the candidate who is thinking about pursuing even higher levels of education. At some point in the lives of, I think most, human entities, they come to a realization they either want or need an education. Something in their lives has changed, causing them to come to a realization, or someone or something has triggered their search.

Let me start by saying there is no definitive guide in existence today that covers all the bases and answers all the questions you may have regarding education: Where, What, Why, When, Who – you know the long list of the W's. There is no place or no one that knows all the answers. Researching is up to the seeker of knowledge. When you successfully complete your educational journey, you will be surprised at the knowledge you have attained throughout your quest. Nobody cares as much as you, so make it good! If you have a question, it is up to you to find the answer. The answer does not know you are looking for it and will not come knocking on your door! Trust me, I do know, as the door didn't knock for me!

The government does not publicize or run marketing campaigns of what they make available to educational facilities and potential students. Few entities know of the grants, scholarships, stipends, loans, etc. backed by the government. When I was in high school, we had counselors that knew all about colleges, requirements, eligibilities, and such things. Do we even have those types of counselors today? I have no idea. There is not a one-stop shop where all this information is made available; the researcher must do their due diligence in finding what they are searching for. Organizations do not generally publicize what offerings they have. I have been a Master Freemason and Shriner for over 23 years, and we do not publish our offerings, but we have them. We discuss those within our ranks. You can liken us to many other organizations across the board – social, honorary, etc. You never know what you will find unless you take the time to look.

Sometimes you have to flip over a lot of rocks in the creek bed to find the crawdad, right? Is it worth the time and trouble? Would you flip over rocks in a creek bed if you knew there was gold under them? Well, education is gold. Scholarships are gold. Grants are gold, right? It is almost like the government and entities have offerings, but they do not want masses of people rushing all at once to get them? You know, like a cattle stampede! They don't want a stampede, so they don't publicize them. Think about this: If there was a 50% off sale at 8:00 am at the Game store, how many people would show up? What time would they start to show up? Would there be a lot of participants? You bet! It would be the same thing if free money were advertised! Do your research.

Where will you go to school? Where would you like to go to school? What is the difference between a public or private institution? Private institutions are generally kept up by alumni and private entities through donations and corporate subsidies. Quite a few of them may also be non-accredited regionally. What does that mean? That means they do not get money from the government like public and/or regionally accredited institutions: i.e. grants, scholarships, and/or financial aid supported by the government. Parents with more money can often send their kids to these. It's not written in stone, but it is in general. Public institutions generally offer the best deals for lower-income parents and/or lower-income students. Public institutions offer a myriad of other money offering programs.

Well, I should have mentioned taxes first, I think, but I will briefly toss them in here. One of the deciding factors of what a student can get depends on taxes. Each year, all of us in the United States fill out tax forms relative to the money we have made, right? Well, are you a dependent of your parents, or are you filing taxes on your own as an independent? This matters if you are seeking to get money for the low-income level. Do your research. You may want to change your filing status and start your educational journey next year after you have made some changes. The system is made to assist you as a taxpayer. Why not research the specifications and use the system for what it is for? Make sense?

There are community colleges, technical schools, and charter-related schools that offer Associate degrees. There are colleges and universities that offer BA, BS, MS, Ed.S., Ph.D., and Ed.D. Programs. Some offer a few choices of those, and some offer many. How high do you propose to go? Well, you generally have to start out small at first. You get one degree, then another, then another. That is the general way to progress. One degree at a time. You never know what might happen in your life, so you don't bite off more than you can chew, right? One at a time.

There are generally Predominantly White Institutions (PWIs) and Historically Black Colleges and Universities (HBCUs). Which one is for you? Well, any of them are for anyone! There is nothing to keep you out of any of them, regardless of your race or creed. Research the institution you are interested in. They all do not offer the same programs. They all do not have the same career recruiters when you graduate. They all do not offer the same grants and/or scholarships. They have quite a few differences, too many to list here.

Do your research. You can research and find: retention rates; acceptance rates; crime rates; and many other statistics if they are important and pertain to you. Some schools have a myriad of student-related activities, and others have fewer. Some schools are in the downtown areas of large cities, while others may be in suburbs or in the middle of nowhere. What is important to you?

Ask around. Find other students, past or present, and seek their opinions. What do they have to say about the institution you are thinking about? Don't just believe the press or the hype; get real up-to-date opinions. A lot can change on a college campus within a single year. Schools sometimes spend a lot of money advertising and marketing programs. What is the purpose of the school marketing the *cons* of their institution? There is no purpose, nor would they like to mention those. There is no perfect educational facility. Not that I have ever seen or heard of. Some are better than others, and some I guess are worse than others. Which one suits you for your purpose?

If you don't like snow and the winter climate, then don't go to a state where it is cold nine months out of the year. If you want to get a degree and transition into the military, then find a college where the military recruits at a high level. Which branch of the military are you interested in? All colleges do not fulfill all branches; some branches are stronger than others in certain areas. Are you interested in being recruited by the government after graduation? Which branch of the government? Some schools have higher career success rates than others. Some big-name industry entities recruit at certain schools. Do your research. Just because you go to school in a certain area does not mean you have to stay in that area in a career. I would think the key here is to plan ahead, if some of your plans just don't seem to work out. We call that life. If you are young, you will come to that realization. It is better to realize it early on than later.

Okay, so we have covered some of the bases of researching before you start your education. Now let's discuss a few things to research after you get started. A lot of these topics and categories meld into each other. It is up to the reader to see some of the parallels and how this all ties up into a package for student success. Think about some of the things we have just gone over regarding research. Toward the end of some programs, your last couple of semesters, you may be asked or you may have the option of taking an internship course. Give this a little thought. You have been in the degree program for three years and by this time you should have a really good idea of what you like about your program and what you don't like in relation to career titles you may be applicable for once you graduate. What do you like to do? Do you want a sit-down job or an active job? Do you want a programming career where you sit 8 hours a day? Do you want a supervisory position? Do you want to be a leader or a follower? There are a lot of pathways you could go if you have done your due diligence and gone above and beyond throughout your educational stint.

After your second year, I would start putting together a resume. A resume of your exploits while in your degree program. Remember, you are going to go above and beyond, right? You are going to mention the technical papers you have written. You are going to mention the internship you have successfully completed. You are going to mention the solo projects you have been involved in as well as the team projects you have been a member of and successfully completed. You are going to mention the organizations you are a member of related to your field or area specialty or specialties. You are going to mention the certificates and/or certifications you currently hold or are planning to pursue after graduation. Oh, I didn't mean to throw all this together in the same paragraph; it is just what came out in my typing and thoughts. Let me split these up in the following paragraphs. I have a little more discussion on the resume, then I have a bit on the differences of certificates and certifications, which can be confusing.

By the end of your second and third year, you should know of career titles you may be applicable for when graduation time comes. Look these up and see what companies are looking for. You can get quite a bit of terminology here just from looking at want ads. These companies will give you a good idea of what exactly they are looking for in their employees. Some of them may even give you some monetary values. They may spell out what hardware and/or software you may be working with, even some specific brands. They may tell you what certifications they are looking for. They will not mention certificates; we will get into that later. They may tell you whether the job is physically on-site and give a location or tell you it is a remote position. There is a lot of information here; don't just scan through it. Listen to what they are saying! They are giving you a gold mine of knowledge. What do you do after you gather this *want ad* information? You tweak your resume to fit the *ad*. You DO NOT have one single resume that fits all jobs you are applying to! You use the language and terminology of the field to fit each application you are replying to! Make sense? Are you paying attention here? Why do a lot of jobs not get filled when qualified people apply to them? Because they do NOT do their research. They get lazy and depressed. "I have this big fancy degree I worked hard to get and I just can't get a job." They write up one single resume, send it out with 100 applications, and they still get no response! Fact!

So, you followed my direction. You have one resume and one application. It all looks good! I reviewed the want ad. I have the correct terminologies for my field of expertise. "I do fit all the information they are asking for in a candidate I just needed a little help with the terminology." All looks good! You send it out or fill the application out online. You get a response. You have an interview date. Good, that is the first step. Step two: Review the company. What do they do exactly? How many employees do they have? How many states are they in? Are they around the world? Do some reading! Find out about them! Take 20 to 30 minutes out of your life. This may come to something.

Is it worth 20 to 30 minutes out of your life to try to land this job by being a great interviewee? I think so! Step three: At the interview, you will no doubt possibly be interviewed by more than one person. At all interviews I have ever been at as a potential employee or even as an interviewer, there is always a question at the end of the interview. "Do you have any questions for us?" During your review in step two, come up with a few questions for the interviewers. MOST interviewees do NOT have any questions! Stand out for MOST of the other interviewees and offer up at least one question. The interviewers will be glad to see you cared enough to review and look up the company. This will be a big plus for your interview. You can even mention that you took the time to review their company and came up with a few questions. Shake everyone's hand!

Do you want to know what step four is? Do you think there is a step four? But my interview is over; why is there a step four? Step four is the step most left out of most all interview processes by the interviewee! You do want to do all you can to get the job, right? Well, this step four is doing all you can to try! It is worth another 5 minutes of your time and/or a dollar or two for a stamp and/or a brief note. Send a *Thank You for the Interview* card or note! Why? Only 5% of the job-seeking population do this! Why? You may possibly be one of many interviews taking place. Why not be the last person on the lips of the interviewees? Stand out from the rest of the candidates! Is it worth doing all you can to try and get the job?

Okay, I mentioned above I would discuss the differences of certificates and certifications. Now is that time. If you noticed, I said that certifications might be delineated within industry job placement want ads. Certifications are wanted by many corporations and entities within the private sector as well as the public. What are certifications? Certifications, in one manner, are materials prepared and presented by a specific company brand. This company brand puts together study materials and offers exams that they support and present. If you attain the passing score, you are granted the certification. This was how it was done and who did it in the beginning, years back. Now, don't confuse the terminology here. If you do pass the certification exam and/or exams, you will be issued a certificate. You have been granted a certificate for achieving a certification, right?

Now here is where the confusion comes in. Receiving a certificate is not the same as completing exams for a certification. Got that? Let me repeat that! Receiving a certificate is not the same as completing exams for a certification. Successfully completing an exam or exams to achieve a certification is what you want. These are recognized by certain entities that feel they are valuable throughout industry in the private and/or public sector. Got that?

Now you have entities that offer certificates in certain specializations or fields, i.e. Cybersecurity or Cyber Security for example. This is where you take a designated structure of materials or courses; you pass them and you are given a certificate. A certificate is not the same as a certification! So, you ask, is a certificate viable? There are a few different scenarios where they are viable.

You may be in a college degree program, and that institution and division also offer certificates for human entities taking a few courses that will lead to a certificate. This example is like killing two birds with one stone. If you are already in a degree program, why not graduate with your degree and get the addition of a free certificate? You earned it, right? You took those courses, right?

In another example, there is something called professional development. You hear this term all over the place. In many working sectors of society, to keep your current job, you must complete certain types of training, usually yearly, and this training is called professional development. This is big in education, government, and civil sectors. Nurses, Professors, EMTs, Police, and many others, too many to list, are held accountable by these standards. These can be viable as usually, not always, they are paid for by employers or they pay a high percentage of the cost. They pay for these because you are making yourself more valuable by gaining more knowledge related to your field. Make sense?

In another example, the recipient of these certificates may spend the money to take them, or their employer may partially or fully pay for them to gain more knowledge in their field. Kind of similar to our last example. In our last example, these certificate holders may receive raises for completing this professional development. On the other hand, in some workplaces, the employer may not pay for them nor recognize certificates as a viable resource. The recipient may just seek to get a better knowledge or understanding of a topic they want to know more about and are willing to pay for it themselves. Now, this is only saying: Do your research. Ask employers if a certificate is viable. Ask specialists in the field. Is this a viable expense? Companies and schools can spend a lot of money advertising for certificates. Don't just take the entity's word for it that their certificate is viable; ask the industry. Educational institutions want bodies in seats and often do not make promises of employability. Do your research.

One last tip related to certifications: Most certifications have a time limit. They are only accountable for a certain amount of time before you need an upgrade of sorts. For example, there is a certain certification that is good for three years. During that three-year period, you are expected to take the next certification and pass it. This passing allows you to keep the previous certification as well as the one you just passed. Then, so on and so on, every three years. Now, pay attention! The dates of passing and achieving these certifications are critical! If you miss the three-year deadline by a day, you will lose the previous certifications you held. If you are nine years in and on your third certification and you miss that anniversary date, you will lose all three previous certifications you struggled to achieve.

## Tam of the Scholar

Why the Tam? This hat or cap is the one you are  seeking if you are in a college degree program. As you see, it has no tassel; the tassel is the signature of the graduate. If you are reading this compilation of ideas I am proposing here in this writing, you surely have not yet graduated. If this writing were relative to the graduate, it would have the addition of a golden tassel.

You are the leader of your destiny. You are the single entity that will be held accountable for your actions. Everything you do as a student on a college campus, either positively or negatively, is recorded in documentation. When coming to a physical campus or completing coursework online, you complete and sign documentation. Documentation tells you what is required, what is expected, and what is not acceptable. Claiming ignorance is not accepted as an excuse on a college campus. Remember reading earlier that you are expected to know your campus? Well, this alludes to this category. All educational facilities have prepared and documented what is called a student handbook. It is the responsibility of the student to read this handbook and understand the implications of following directions and doing what is expected as well as ignoring the directions and suffering penalties. Read this handbook.

A lot has changed over the years in post-secondary education. In the early years of Yale, Harvard, and other institutions of that time, a student could be expelled from a University for the naivest forms of cheating. Expulsion. Expulsion, and you would not get back in. This expulsion went on your record and you could not apply to any other institution without them reviewing your expulsion. This was a big deal at that time and still is to this day, a big deal. When you accept an invitation to enroll and register for courses, it is expected that you know right from wrong. If you do not know, you better ask for direction.

This is not generally a negotiable issue; cheating is cheating. This is spelled out in the student handbook as well as every syllabus you review. This is one reason each semester you fill out and submit a syllabus acknowledgment form for each course. This submission documents that you have read and agree with the syllabus. If you do not fill out and submit this, generally in the first two weeks of a course, you run the risk of being removed from that course for non-compliance.

These days you can still run the risk of expulsion and/or suspension. If suspension is the chosen penalty, it usually suspends the student from taking any courses for a full year. This also goes on the student record forever. It all boils down to: Are you willing to risk your name, honor, and reputation for cheating? Once you are branded a cheater, you will always be branded a cheater. Why cheat? Sometimes a student gets tired and lazy and just copies and pastes from the internet to fulfill an assignment. Is this cheating? Yes, you are taking the words of someone else and turning them in as your own. This is cheating and plagiarism. It does not matter if you are writing a paper, an essay, or a thesis and you denote a reference to these words in the reference section. If these words are directly copied from what that author said, you are cheating and plagiarizing. You must take what that author said and put it into your own words and make it your own. If it is copied and pasted, they are not your words.

If you don't try it, you won't get caught up in it! If you never cheat, you don't have to worry about ever getting caught cheating. If you start out with just cheating small, you may soon find you run the risk of getting caught for larger issues. Don't put that thought in your system, and you don't have to worry about it. This involves psychological processes within our makeup. Freud would have a lot to say here, I would guess. If you start stealing small things, you might find through the years you end up stealing bigger things or more things. If you don't start it, you don't have to worry about it, right?

Honor, integrity and pride. When you strip away our physicality that is all we are and all we have. You can't just register and enroll in a course and acquire these three things. You either have them or you don't have them. They have either been instilled in each of us through our relationships throughout our lives. Someone, someone's, something and or something's imbedded these into us or not. Some human entities think they have them, some wish they had them, and some portray themselves to have them. If you see something that is wrong, justify and minimize it, and turn your head, is it your problem or responsibility. Can or will your conscience affect or effect you? Maybe or maybe not? Only each one of us know the answer, it is within ourselves, our being. Are all of us intertwined in this world together or are we separated? I can't give you that answer. I would guess we all try to survive, try to do the right thing, and try to be a positive light in someone else's eye, or not. I would think everyone would rather be known in a positive way than a negative. What do you want to be, how do you want to be remembered, and what slogan do you want on your stone, when your physical presence is gone? Something to think about.

It seems as though I have spent a lot of time on this topic or maybe it is better said to be an idea. This idea of honor, integrity and pride, *ideas or ideals*. Each of us know or at least think we know what is inside of us and what we would propose to do in certain situations if those situations arose. I would guess anyway. All I am really trying to say is to be the best you can be and don't start something you may not be able to stop. The human brain is a complex thing, the only way I can explain its composition in layman's terms. Being more expansive with big words and terms has no viability here. Maybe an example? If you are married and you cheat with someone else. Once you realize you have easily gotten away with it. Does that leave you open to doing it again, maybe? If you lie on a job application and get the job. What if someone decides to research your application and finds issues? Is it worth losing a high paying position? Once you lie, will you always lie? I guess that remains to be seen though each of us. If you sell something by weight and put your finger on the scale. Will you always put your finger on it, since it worked the first time?

How about an example: When I was younger I was in line at a department store. For some reason I had a twenty dollar bill in my pocket, not my billfold. I was standing in line. I reached into my pocket and the twenty fell out onto the floor. The guy behind me immediately stepped on it to cover it up with his foot. I saw it fall and looked around. I saw the guy out his foot on the twenty. I asked the people around me if they saw anything fall from my pocket. One of the girls said "yes it's under his foot". She pushed the guy and his foot came off the twenty. I thanked her, reached down and picked up the twenty. It wasn't her twenty was it? Why did she say anything?

How about another example: This is a little long. I was in a course for my BS degree, a teacher education class. Our professor mentioned that tomorrow we were having a midterm exam. All the students as well as myself curiously looked at each other. We mentioned we were not ready for a midterm exam and we needed more time. He said the midterm will be tomorrow and that he would not be there to proctor the exam that he would have a replacement professor stand in for him during his absence, but the exam would stay as scheduled. He said "Now, if all of you stick together as a class and decide to not take the exam, I cannot give a passing grade to any of you, as all of you would have a zero. You all would just put your name and date on the exam and turn it in". He kind of smiled while he was talking and repeated what he had said! "If NONE of you take the exam then you will all have the same grade a zero!"

Proceed to the next day, midterm exam day. One of the other professors handed out the midterm exams to each of us. We all looked at each other, and asked each other what we were going to do. The professor was curious and asked what we were doing. We told him what our professor had said. He smiled and said "well, what are you all going to do"? There were about twenty of us, we all signed and dated our exams and turned them in. We all waited until all of us had turned them in, then we all got up, and left the classroom. This was Friday. Monday came, we were all sitting in the classroom. Our regular professor was there. He was in front of class smiling and said "well, this is the first time I have ever been taken up on my offer for the whole class to get together and not take the midterm exam. I have offered many times and you are the first class. Now, if you remember, I said specifically, that as long as all of you stuck together, signed, dated and turned in your exams with no completed answers you all would have the same grade. That I could not really fail anyone specifically you all would get a zero for the exam. Now, did I not say this?" We all nodded and said "yes"!

Then he smiled and said "well we have ran into a problem! One of you felt guilty of not taking the exam Friday and came to me over the weekend and asked if he could take the exam. If you remember, I said all of you would have to stick together, so apparently that was not so, as all of you did not stick together. So, I could either let this one person take the exam and pass him if he only answered one question and give a zero to all the rest of you, therefore all of you fail the exam other than him, or I cannot give him the exam and reschedule tomorrow for all of you to retake the exam, and I propose to do the latter. Tomorrow we all will be taking the midterm exam. He was a good and fair professor that was in his rights if he gave a zero to all of us except the one who felt guilty and contacted him. We had him for many classes. We really missed him when he died.

On a similar note you may run into a one-word term when coming to a college campus, that term is ethics. Ethics may be something we take for granted that we really don't think about, but we know it exists, kind of like knowing *right* from *wrong*. We think and hope everyone understands and comprehends right from wrong, but do we take it for granted that everyone has been taught it? I think we often do, and sometimes we get a realistic smack in the mouth when we see a student get caught up in not knowing or apparently not caring.

In actuality, even the best and most talented of students can sometimes let their guard down and get caught up in unethical situations. One of the topics I am rather familiar with, as I speak of them often in the courses I teach in Cybersecurity, is the three hats of the hacker: The Black, the White, and the Gray. These have often been likened to the western cowboys of early 1900 serials. The guy with the Black hat is the bad guy, the white hat the good guy, and the gray hat sometimes changes sides during the adventure. This pretty much reflects the hats of the hackers, and they follow in parallel with the cowboy serials of old.

In relation to this category, I am talking about the gray hat hacker. The gray hat hacker thinks and reasons in his or her mind they are doing something for the common good, but in fact, what they are doing is still wrong and probably breaking a law. Take for instance a volunteer within a political party. They have access to certain information. If this information disappeared or was removed, it might enable their political candidate to win. So, they justify in their mind they need to remove it as their candidate is what they think is the best. They think their candidate is the best for the job and, therefore, they remove the information. Well, even though they reason and believe they are doing the right thing, they are still breaking a law and will be given a penalty if found out. Basically, they are a bad guy thinking they are doing a good deed, which is unethical.

Many times a student gets tired and lazy. Maybe they are in their last semester before graduating and just want to graduate and be done. They think, just this once and I will be fine. Just this once. Well, all it takes is once. Getting caught one time can put your college career and/or your career future in a bad position. A position you may not easily get out of or may not have removed from your college transcript. All we really have is our honor, integrity, and good name. The rest is just dust and a lot of water. Have you ever heard 'Ashes to ashes, Dust to dust'?

Another mention in this category is: *Don't judge a book by its cover.* Have you ever heard that? In the educational realm we are told that students want to see someone who looks like them in their classrooms. I can understand that point, however, sometimes it is just not feasible. Sometimes the population pool of the candidates with their right credentials for the position are just not enough. A lot of this has to do with the different cultures and how they view education. Sometimes the government steps in and delegates what percentage of one race or creed or other has to be hired. Kind of like affirmative action and sometimes it is in reverse. This also brings to me another point.

Think about cultures that may be different than yours. How about a story? You never really realize but there are many Eastern Asian countries as well as creeds. Too many to list here, this isn't a lesson on Eastern Asia. One of my best friends I met while at flight school many years ago is from China. In China in their early school years they spend a lot of time learning about Asian and the many Asian cultures. Just like when I was in Arkansas when I was in junior high school we took classes in Arkansas history.

Anyway, several few years ago my friend came for a visit. We went to a really large restaurant. In that restaurant there were many tables of customers and quite a few of the customers were Asian. My friend would point to each person and tell me the country they were from and what district or dialect they would speak without even hearing their voice: Korean, Chinese, Mongolian, Japanese, etc. You get the picture. He even mentioned that in each of those countries that there could be many different language dialects. That was pretty cool. I never knew there were so many differences in just the Eastern Asian culture.

You can receive anything with an open mind. Open your mind and you will not believe what knowledge you might attain. You might even change some current opinions you have. Did you know it is impolite in some countries to offer your right hand for a handshake? Some may get offended. On certain days during the year some people do not eat anything all day as a form of fasting. In some countries it is impolite to look at someone in the eye if you are speaking to them. In some countries woman wear veils over their faces. The list goes on. Sometimes we might offend someone and not know. We can't know every custom, right?

At the beginning of every semester I look out at my class and wonder about everyone in the seats. I can see the physical things of what they look like, their race, creed, color and appearance. I can't see their mental side or their internals, right? I wonder where they came from. Why are they here? What is their family like? I wonder about students just as much as they probably wonder about me.

I mentioned in my biography that before I was 18 years old my family and I moved 27 times. After I turned 18 I moved myself quite a few times. I have been around the block a time or two, seen and been a part of quite a few things. Did you know when I was younger I taught gun safety to boy scouts, and was involved in full-contact Tae Kwon Do for many years. I'll bet you didn't know I was once asked if I was interested in cross-country running for the Olympics and wrecked a motorcycle at over 100 miles per hour. I also had a low-rider truck that was involved in Audio competitions. These were just a few highlights, you would be surprised at some of the others as well.

Somewhere around here I still have a whole case of rap and bass CDs that you most of you probably never heard of, but I'll say this: They bring the BASS! The bass in my truck would hit so hard you could stand outside the truck with the window down a few inches and when the woofer drivers compressed it would pull the air out of your lungs and you couldn't draw a breath. You would be surprised at the motorcycles in my garage and those stories. I guess what I am trying to say is that you don't realize what others around you are or have been involved in. The college years are said to be *the best years of your lives* and *you may make friendships that will last for years*, how can you do these things if you don't reach out and ask questions of others around you. You just never know what positive things around you may find to get involved in.

Anyway, how about a story about *judging a book by its cover*? Before I ever thought of going to college one of my best friends was in college up north. One of the times I went to visit her it happened that during that weekend there was a big wine and cheese festival going on in the neighboring county. I was invited to go and everyone the bus was a college senior, except me. The whole time on this bus trip to the festival and back this girl kept staring at my feet. I didn't really think anything about it. We got to the festival, spent the day, got on the bus for the return trip. This girl kept staring at my feet, so I decided I was curious as to why. I asked her "you keep staring at my feet and I was wondering why"? She thought a minute. Now this was an educated young girl, right? She said "you are from Kentucky right"? I said "yes". She said "but you have on shoes. I was always told Kentucky is full of Hillbillies and they don't wear shoes. Do other people in Kentucky wear shoes"? True story.

How about another one? Go to a state up north and ask for sweet tea, they will look at you like you are from another planet and give you some packs of sugar. Go to a state down south and ask for unsweet tea. They will ask you where you are from. Down south we don't drink unsweet tea. Go up to Minnesota and ask for a bottle of pop. They will look at you and ask what is a pop? Go to Alabama and ask for a soda. They will do the same thing. If you ask for a soda pop they will all wonder from what planet you came?

How about one more example. When I was a corporation owner I went with one of my crews to a major city up north. Several of my crew members wore old surplus army coats. It was winter time and cold! Whenever we went into restaurants they would always put us in the back away from everyone else. There was usually 8 or 10 of us at a time. We didn't think much about it, as we always had to ask for sugar packets for our sweet tea anyway. Just another weird thing, right? Well, we got to know some of the people at these restaurants so they finally told us why they would always put us at the back tables away from everyone else. They said that gangs were always an issue up there and that gang colors were a real problem. They said those military surplus army coats were gang color up there and that if a gang had seen my people wearing them it might have become a real problem for a rival gang! I guess that made sense?

So the moral of the stories are *to not judge a book by its cover.* Keep an open mind. Closed minds are a main reason for many of the issues around the world today. All we are is what we are. One day, that is all we will ever be—all of us. Maybe a positive phrase on a tombstone.

In my life, throughout my years, I have come up with a conclusion of sorts. I will end this category with this thought. There are two kinds of people on the earth, as I know it: *When bad things happen.* One of them sits back and says, "Why me? What did I do to deserve this"? And the other one says, "It was about time, I knew it was coming". Which of these people do you want to be?

# Campaign of the Confident

Why the Campaign? This hat is worn by drill sergeants  in all branches of the United States Military, Park Rangers, some State Police, as well as the Canadian Mounted Police. This is a sign of respect and confidence—confidence that you will do what is necessary when the need arises.

You are not in this venture alone. You may feel like you are, but you are not. Let me put it this way: You should not be alone on a college campus. You should not be made to feel like you are alone on a college campus. If you feel that way, maybe you are not on the right campus for you. All physical brick-and-mortar campuses should have social environments on their campus. All should have health specialists for students who get ailments or have depression or anxieties. All should have a Student Government in place. The voice for the student is the Student Regent. That person is a member of the Board of Regents of all colleges and universities. This person is your mouthpiece. This person is the one person on campus charged with bringing student issues forth to the Board of Regents.

Part of this category is confidence—confidence that a college freshman has acquired and exuded to make their degree attempt successful. Let's talk a bit about shyness. Maybe bashfulness is a better-known term? You may not be the potential college candidate who is scared to go out into the public or even weary of taking on a task, as you have no idea at this time in your life what you are capable of accomplishing. Maybe you just have not been put into a situation where you need to prove your competence, confidence, or bravery, right? Sound like you?

Well, let me tell you a story. I am full of stories, just ask my students. "That guy must be 150 years old." So, you may not have read my biography yet, but there I mention growing up and moving around quite a bit before I was 18 years old. I will expand a little as I didn't want to make a ten-page biography, but I do like using examples to get my points across in the writing.

So, I was very shy my whole early life—elementary, junior, and high school. Well, high school not so much. During those years, I would rather a teacher give me a zero for a grade than stand up and give a presentation. When I was little and on the playground, I would get picked on by the other kids. Maybe I was small for my age? I don't recollect. I just didn't seem to fit in for some reason. I wanted people to like me, I just didn't know how to make them. I wasn't taught to be the bully or fight, so that was out of the equation. Our family moved so many times I just never got to make many friends, so maybe that was the designating factor? I still don't know.

I always seemed to make it a point to tell the teacher ahead of time I was taking a zero on the presentation, as I didn't even want my name to be called, so I wasn't involved in some sort of scene. Boy, has that changed now! You would not even recognize me now. Once I got out of the general education schools, quite a few years later, I decided to go to college, as you will read about in previous paragraphs here.

Like I mentioned earlier, I was really good at helping and assisting other students who didn't catch onto coursework as well as I did. The professors goaded me to get more education past my AS degree, a two-year degree in computer electronics. I enrolled in the BS degree program of Career and Technical Education (CTE). This program was for students who wanted to be teachers when they grew up and for current teachers in the field who wanted to learn how to better do their careers as a vocational, technical school, or high school vocational technology teacher—the methods, materials, and psychologies related to students in the classroom. Well, it seemed as though every class I had was bombarded with presentation assignments. Well, this degree program was for a teacher, right? What do teachers do all day? Guess? Stand up and teach.

So, in the first semester, I was like, how am I going to get out of this? I must be in the wrong program. How was I talked into this? OMG. So, I struggled for a time, but I completed things! I came to a realization! Hence, the reason for this example. Are you listening and paying attention? Are you? Well, here it comes! "Everyone else in the class has to do it too! Everyone! Is there something different you have to do? No! It is that simple! Everyone else has to do it." Billions of past students have done it too. I will give you a few tidbits of information since I did it too!

Nobody in that class cares. Nobody in that class is going to heckle or make fun of you because they do not want you to do it to them. They may be looking at you, so as to be kind, so you don't feel you are alone, or they may just look and ignore you, but all in all, they don't care. They are as curious about you as you are about them. If they are not a pro at speaking, they are looking to see how you do. They may follow your lead. They may have no idea either of how to proceed, right? They are not professionals at it. What did I say before about *practice*? That *practice makes perfect*. I promise they are not going to get a straw and blow a spit wad at you, as they don't want to come sailing towards them. This is part of what is good about post-secondary education. Respect and kindness you sometimes don't see during secondary education. In higher levels of education, there are things called respect, ethics, and discipline. So, *don't sweat the small stuff*—throughout your life, there will be plenty of large things to sweat; now is not the time nor the place.

I would have to mention one final thing for this category and that is: know your limitations. We all want to do our best, right? Sometimes we just take on too many projects and we just can't seem to handle them, right? Have you ever done that? Have you ever had the best of intention and said you would be happy to accomplish a task and it seemed as though you just didn't have enough time to complete it? I think we all have at one time or another. I can honestly say I have. Sometimes we feel can handle a large load, but can we really? Sometimes we think if I just add one more class for a several semesters I can graduate early. Well, sometimes that might be right, maybe. Sometimes, just we seem to just overthink things. My advice and something I have always done, and I'm not perfect but like to be prepared. Make a list of pros and cons and see which side of the list wins out. If I take that extra class will I still get the high grades I want or am I taking the chance of degrading my GPA, right? You need to always keep in the back of your mind your GPA. Too low of a GPA and we might be removed from the program. Too low of a GPA we might be removed from a scholarship or grant. There is a reason someone many years ago came up with the idea that a full-time student should have 12 credit hours a semester, right? Everything we do has an affect or an effect on something else, right? For every action there is a reaction. That's physics, right? We can prepare for every day in our lives but some things you just can't prepare for. Things just happen and sometimes we don't understand why they happen, they just happen to all of us. *Good things happen to bad people and bad things happen to good people.* Sometimes there just is no logical answer to it!

If you have ever had me in a class you know we may get on any topic. In my opinion an education does not have to have a topic or title. My job is to help students as best I can. If you have a question about 'under-water basket weaving' ask it, I just might have an answer and an explanation, right? I write like I speak. I give examples whenever I can and time allows. Isn't it better to have too much information than not enough?

How about this question. If and or when the student GPA gets low, who is responsible for telling you or reminding you? Is that a good question? Well, the short answer is things do *fall through the cracks*, sometimes, right? That just happens. There is a lot going on at an educational facility behind the scenes, you may not realize. Most facilities have initiatives in place and responsibilities doled out but the true fact of the matter is, you the student are the sole responsibility of your GPA, knowing what it is, how it got there, and what you need to do to fix it, if it need fixing. I mentioned earlier in this writing, nobody is going to knock on your door, to present you with a lot of realizations, you should know as a student in the first place. Hence, the need for the time and energy I have spent here.

One last item for here. We hear a lot about *fake news*. I don't think I have to go into a lot of detail here, I think we all know what fake news is, where it comes from, and why it exists. Parallel with *fake news* is: Know what you are talking about. Whatever career choice you propose to enter into or whatever social event you attend, you need to *talk the talk and walk the walk*. If you just graduated with a degree in Cybersecurity, you should know about it, right? You should know the lingo and be able to carry on a conversation within that realm of expertise. You should be somewhat of an expert on that topic, you would think, I would think. Surely you paid enough attention in class that you passed with flying colors, got the degree, and here you are searching for a career. Maybe you already have one and are at the Christmas party mingling, talking to your compatriots. They expect you to be on the same wave as them. They expect you to know what you are talking about, right?

Time for an example. I will also add this: Do your research. Don't just take the word of someone else, sometimes you just need to go the extra step, and find out the answer for yourself, if might just be *fake news*. Anyway, A few years into my corporation we had a service call to a local company that bought a network of computers from us and we had previously setup a complete network on several floors. I don't remember the issue, but I am sure it was simple. If you get involved with the realm of the IT field tech and service level agreements (SLAs) you quickly realize that in general you see the same 10 issues time and time again and every now and then you see something odd that you have to dig a little deeper to resolve. Anyhow, we had resolved the issue and it was around 11:45 in the afternoon, just before lunchtime. We were closing out the call and speaking with the manager, who was the typical customer and user who depended upon us, her computer guys, for accurate information, right?

Just before we go out the door the manager is going around to each office and telling the staff to make sure they all are done with their work before lunch as all their computers must be turned off and shut down before lunch. My tech and I looked at each other wondering what was happening. Why was she having everyone turn off their computers before lunch? What was the deal? Are you ready for it, the punchline? Well, we asked her…

Here it comes: She said because "Everyone in the United States goes to lunch from 12:00 to 1:00 and all computers need to be off from 12:00 to 1:00 so they can go to lunch too, at the same time as computers must have rest along with the people". OMG...She was serious! Needless to say we were about to die laughing, but she was serious! She wasn't one of those people who laugh along with you she would have been offended. Anyway, we asked "Who told you that"? She said some tech in the past had told her that and she had been sticking to it for years. So, my point here is: Because she was told something wrong, and believed it, those poor employees had been making sure their PCs were off from 12:00 to 1:00 every day for years, because computers had to rest for lunch along with the people. That was funny but true! If you ever become an IT field technician, you will have many stories like this. Along those same lines, give your customers good advice as you will surely see them again.

## Propeller Beanie of the Happy

Why the Propeller Beanie? This is the fun hat, the

happiness hat. This is my, *I am here to have a good time* hat. Just look at the hat, and it needs no explanation. This might be likened to a clown's wig or a big green ST. Patty's Day hat. Flashy and attention grabbing, right?

Don't let the search for knowledge overwhelm you. A college degree is a big deal. It is nothing to be scared of. Students apply and are accepted every semester. Students leave home at the beginning of every semester from all over the world. Some students for the first time in their lives. Along with all the things I have mentioned before for your success as a college freshman, you also need to have a little bit of fun. A little bit of happiness. What have we always been told about a college education throughout the ages? "A well-rounded or balanced education." Another one is "The best years of our lives". Do these sound familiar? I heard them while I was going to college.

How can you have a well-rounded or balanced education when all of it is 100% work? It just doesn't seem like you can to me. There needs to be some interwoven fun, joy, and pleasure in there somewhere. But NOT too much, this is where the first-year college freshman often runs into trouble, and it sometimes ends their college and degree quest. Don't let your first-year experience turn into your GPA downfall! Whether on a scholarship or someone is paying cash. It can be quite a chore to recover.

What is fun anyway? What do you consider pleasure? What makes you happy? This can be a rather difficult proposition, right? What makes me happy, for example, is seeing others happy. Of course, we all have hobbies and or things we like to do: Ride roller coasters; Eat ice cream; Go to concerts; etc. That is one side of fun, happiness, and pleasure. That is the *getting, taking, and receiving* side, right? There is another side *giving, charity, and philanthropy*, right? Volunteering might be a better and more understandable word? Some people get more out of giving than they do out of receiving. Some people just don't need a pat on the back to keep them going; some just want to feel they have a purpose and are needed.

When I was in Flight school, there was a women's religious group that came once a month on a Saturday and provided a home-style lunch to all the flight students who attended. Now, you need to realize that the students at this college were from all around the world and were from all races and creeds. Some were thousands of miles away from home. So, in reality, this was a big deal for some students and not so big for others, but it was appreciated by all who attended. This was a story of the community of neighbors reaching out to us, which relates to our conversation here, but here we are again, receivers and takers of pleasure. But it provides a point that the community outside the college you attend, I am sure, has the same intentions of wanting to be a part of the future of student success. Make sense?

Some college towns are smaller than others, and some are larger than others. Some colleges have a huge relationship with the outside, and others not so much. Who is to say the college freshman needs to rely on the college to provide relationships with the outside communities? There may be some that you do not realize exist, so it is your responsibility to ask, is it not? If something does not exist, maybe it is your 'calling' to search it out and provide a pathway for future students.

Maybe? Just because something does not exist does not mean you cannot be the first to make it happen. Somebody has to start everything. Things just don't happen by chance. Like I mentioned before about 'a knock on the door'. Sometimes you need to do the knocking! You might be surprised at what is behind the door. The door that you knocked on.

The same is true with organizations. Maybe there is an organization you are interested in that has no sponsorship on your campus. Maybe they once had sponsorship and it just seemed to fizzle out and was put aside for lack of representation and interest. In my second year of college, there were quite a few of us in technology who wanted to belong to something. We didn't know what, we just knew we worked hard, we worked together, and we wanted to join something that would recognize our efforts. We spoke around to professors in our area and found that in the past our department was heavily involved in an honors fraternity, Epsilon Pi Tau. An honors fraternity for technology students. To make a long story short, we had the Gamma Mu designation reinstated, and we had if I remember correctly 15 or so members. I was the first President of that honors fraternity for two years. I am not sure today if there is involvement within that or if it was put back to the side once again. I was back there about ten years ago, and the glass case we purchased to provide our exploits and brochures were proudly still being displayed there. In remembrance, I have an Epsilon Pi Tau (EΠT) hat and a flag to remember those proud days.

A big word you hear a lot on a lot of college campuses, the radio, and the television is 'volunteer,' right? It appears as though everyone needs some volunteers. It may not be in your city or town, it may not be in your state. I can promise you, if you look, you will find an unlimited supply of organizations and or people asking for volunteers. What need is great in your area? How about something related to elderly people or animals?

Do you realize that the majority of elderly people seldom have anyone visit them? Do some research, look up the statistics? There is your niche. How about a local animal shelter? Animals are always looking for a friend, and all they want is a kind word and a pat on the head, and they will be your loyal friend for life. If you are looking for something to give you a 'Propeller Beanie' feeling, then those may be for you.

The point here is to get some happiness from these years you are planning to devote to an education. What is the saying, *All work and no play make Jack a dull boy*? Well, that can be true, right? Get some enjoyment out of life. These are supposed to be some of the best years of your life. Use them to their full advantage. Don't let them use you, you use them!

I have to add some information that is very important, and is usually at the top of the list, but I could not add it to any of the other 'hat' categories without being confusing. These are topics I will combine: Safety, Security, and Health.

As far as safety and security make it a point to know your campus and where things are. I mentioned this earlier. Know your campus. Know where the safe places are. Know who to contact if you need someone, ASAP! All campuses are not the same. Do your research.

Health, now that is a big topic. Most of us know about physical health, Band-Aids and medicines, right? Well, if not I think we should. I want to spend some time talking about the other side of health, mental health. Mental health is on the inside, something we cannot see and we often take for granted. Everyone is different, so the behavioral specialist and psychologists tell us. We all can react differently to the same scenarios. There is no one-stop tell all book that covers everything. Bad things happen to good people and good things happen to bad people. Sometimes you just don't understand how some reacted to a given situation and no matter how many times you mull it over in your mind you may never come up with what you believe to be a logical make-sense answer.

All of us, students, faculty, staff, we are all human entities. We all deal with things differently. Some of us can take higher levels of sadness and others may only take lower levels of sadness. Most of us do not know the level we can take until we are already intertwined in it. You just don't or won't know until it happens. This is one time when we can truly say *we are all in this together*. We all get subjected to negative issues. One of the most prolific in my mind is dealing with death. Nobody likes to talk about it or be reminded of it. Death is around all of us and seems to just sit back and wait its turn. We would like to think that death takes holidays, but I don't think he/she does. The younger we are the less death we have to deal with, and that is a good thing. The more we move up the ladder with age the more we see, and we don't like it, none of us like it.

All through this book I have given examples of things I have seen throughout my life to hopefully give a little better idea and understanding behind the do's and don'ts we all read or are told to read when we are college students. I could give a lot of examples here of death I have dealt with over the last few years but I think you get the picture. I don't like to think about it but I know that these things are part of what has made me what I am today. All things we endure make us who we are, right? If life throws us a curve we catch it and throw it right back. Life is full of curves we don't see up in the road ahead, we get into the curve, our brain tells us to slow down, then when we get close to the end of the curve we see up ahead, we accelerate and come out of it. That is our job, to accelerate and come out of it accelerating toward the finish line. It is our job to make it to the finish line.

I mentioned we don't like to talk about death, generally. It makes us sad. But I will say this: Why are there support groups where things like this are discussed freely and openly if talking about it does not help? Then I would say, talking about it must help! If it didn't help, then nobody would show up, right? That's what I would think too. I think sometimes sad things need to be talked about too.

I am rambling on here, my point is: We are all the same. We understand these things happen. It seems easier to me if I talk about these things. I know we all want to hold them inside but I don't think it is good to hold them in. I think personally it is better to talk about some of the issues that are bothering us. Most campuses have health departments and counselors that can help us deal with issues that bother us. If you have an issue that may cause problems for you completing your work and assignments let someone know. Let someone know. Let someone know. This goes back to the earlier conversation I had here about ESP. None of us on the college campus have ESP. If you have issues you must open up and let us know.

If you have issues like these don't wait until you cannot dis-enroll in a course without paying a bill. Don't wait until after the allowable withdrawal date to earn a 'W' instead of an 'F'. There is also a letter grade of 'I' for Incomplete if that may be of assistance to you during a time of issue. Don't procrastinate. This was in a previous conversation too. Don't wait and don't procrastinate.

Sometimes something you think is a minor mental issue or hiccup in your life could creep up on you and before you realize it, is a major issue you feel is overwhelming. *Don't let things overwhelm you*. These college years are supposed to be the best years of your lives, don't let them become the worst. Control the things you can control and try to deal with the things you cannot control. Always remember, you are no different than anyone else. We all deal with things every day, some are positive and some are negative. If you need help ask for it.

It is rather easy to find a faculty or staff member on campus that you may have a good rapport with. Just give a brief mention in passing and you might be surprised at what you can strike up. You might be surprised to find someone just like you. You just have to look. You just have to keep a somewhat open mind and look. Remember when you were little, you were out walking, you stop at the street corner and whomever was holding your hand said something? Remember that? What did they say? What did they say before you crossed the street? Was it: *Stop, look and listen. Stop, look and listen* and make these college years the best of your lives.

I have said before college years are supposed to be the best years of our lives, so years of graduates tell us. There are good experiences and bad I am sure. I have to give one last good experience of mine before I end. Let me give a little background to set it up first. There is a country western singer called George Strait. This was about 30 years ago when I was in flight school in Alabama. If you look up George you will see is the picture of the flawless 'cowboy', the pressed Wrangler jeans, the fresh ironed long sleeve shirt, the Justin Ropers, the big buckle and cowboy hat. At the end of his concerts he holds his hat up and waves at the crowd.

Now to the story. Every other weekend a bunch of my college buddies and I would head off to Panama City Florida, it was pretty close to our school. One particular weekend it was spring break. We decided to pack up and go for the day. Several of us were driving vehicles, this was before cell phones. We were about 10 minutes from Panama, and one of my buddies was in the front vehicle and flagged us to pullover. We pulled over and he said he had to stop for a few minutes. He got out of his truck with some hangers of clothes. We all had on shorts and tee shirts for the summer spring break heat. He went into the bathroom, came out, and you would swear it was George Strait! Our buddy looked a lot like him to begin with, let alone the pressed jeans, long sleeve ironed shirt, boots, buckle at hat. What was he thinking? It was HOT!

So, we give our buddy a hard time and drive on. We get to Panama and the hotel we are at is having a huge Karaoke system setup and the pool is full with hollering partying spring breakers. It was off-the-hook or off-the-chain depending on what you call it. So, some of us walk down the beach and some of us stay behind. So, I and some others walk down the beach. About an hour later we head back to the hotel down the beach. The closer we get the louder the party is and the louder the Karaoke. They had some huge speakers! I mean huge! So, the closer we get, we recognize one of the songs. It was a George Strait song. Then we ask ourselves what that awful 'cat squalling' voice is trying to sing those George Strait lyrics. OMG. You had to be there! Anyway, we get there and the crown is going wild and our buddy is on stage singing. If you can call that 'cat squalling' singing? He was awful, and couldn't carry a tune in a bucket! But the crown was partying and apparently didn't care, right? Well, not really, they were trying to get him off stage! But he wouldn't leave! Finally, after like three songs he finally held his hat in the air and waved to the crown and they cheered and he came down from the stage.

We asked him how that happened and what he had done to get up on stage. He said the Karaoke people were curious as to why he was dressed the way he was and he told them he was there for spring break and he was a back-up singer for George Strait, and that he knew all the songs, and was ready to sing. Apparently, the people believed him and put him on stage and after the first song realized there was something wrong with that picture. So, the story doesn't end here.

So, we all applaud him for his 'whatever you call it' and get in our vehicles and head back to school. One of my other buddies rides with the 'cowboy'. It was about a two hour ride. We get back and our buddy riding with the 'cowboy' says don't you guys ever do that to me again! The Karaoke people made a recorded cassette or the singing and the 'cowboy' enjoyed it so much and was so proud of himself he played it in the truck the whole way back! Anyway, I just had to mention this as out of hundreds of funny stories this one will always stick in my mind. Several of these guys we keep in touch all the time, no matter what country or state we are in. We still talk and laugh about the 'cat squalling' and our friend the 'cowboy'. My college years were surely some of the best years of my life.

## Dunce of the Labelled

Why the Dunce? This hat or cap was often given to the

student in a class who was disruptive in class. This student was often associated with the slow-to-learn student. These two students were often thrown into the same label, which we now know to be wrong as just because a student now-a-days is a little slower at grasping the points in classroom instruction does not also mean they are disruptive. Neither, does that mean to associate the slow-to-learn students as dysfunctional, handicapped, or disabled. Although, early in educational history many labels were often gathered by one or more

derogatory or negative labels. Although, as we all know there are always exceptions to every rule. Do your research.

You may have gathered by now that this is not one of the hats a student needs to be successful. I felt it needed to be added as a topic of this writing as a notice for a potential student that may be labeled in this category. Maybe you had low scores on entrance exams, a lower than average GPA, or a multitude of other reasons. Don't let how you are treated or take offense to negative labels you may acquire along your pathway to educational success. It is the outcome that matters, not the incoming labels!

Although, I remember when I was little being told by my parents to go stand in the corner, when I was thought to be pestering my younger sisters. Which of course, I was I assure you. I still see this today, where parents call it "time out".

I guess what I am trying to say here is that you cannot know everything! Isn't that the reason a student registers in degree programs, to learn new things. To get guidance and direction to learn new things they would have never just sat down and learned themselves. We all can go to the book store and buy a book and read it. We all can go to a library and pull a book from the shelf and sit down a read it. Isn't the purpose of having an educator, a guide, a conductor of sorts, to associate that book reading with real life, so the student can understand the why's and how's and their relationships to life.

Things come easy to some students and thinks come difficult to some students. If we are all products of our environments, then that would be a natural assumption. Some students grasp concepts with ease and some take more time to comprehend. Sometimes it takes more time to put thoughts together. Most students I have ever had in class have a fear of embarrassment. Maybe some students just want to put all their thoughts together before speaking, instead of correcting themselves as they go. Just like a speaker prepares for his presentation, right? Nobody wants to stand in front of a crowd, and speak, and look like they do not know what they are talking about, right?

As a student don't think you are supposed to know the answers to everything. You don't know everything or you would not need an education. Someone is paying for you to get an education. You need to get the best education you can receive. Of course we do often get plagued with stereotypes or labels. Maybe we not need think of them as negative or hindrance labels maybe they can be used as opportunities.

If you do have a need for assistance in your learning, or have been clinically diagnosed with some type of learning disability all post-secondary educational facilities have assistive learning offices for that. If it is available to you and it will assist you, why not take advantage of it and use it. There are so many things in our lives that are not advertised and we often do not know about, but I assure you, there things are available, and if it will help you to learn, use them, that is why they have been provided. I assure you, professors have no problem going out of their way if needed to help any students to learn! It may be their job, but most professors I have come into contact with throughout my life as a student as well as an educator, would think nothing less of you if you needed more out-of-their-way help from them. They would actually think more of you as you realized you needed help, you sought out that help, and asked them for that help.

What is the old saying "There is no thing as a stupid question". What is the other one "The only stupid question, is a question unasked". Educators want students to ask question in their classrooms. This is how educators gauge the responsiveness and participation of their students. It is your right as a student to get answers if you need them.

Then we have the other hand, that of the educator. Does every educator know everything about the topic they teach? I sincerely doubt they are the all-knowing or omniscient of all they have surveyed. Seriously. We are all humans too, I assume. We are not infallible either. We all go through professional development each year too, we continue to be students even after we have achieved higher degrees and titles within the educational realm. If we knew everything why would we need to continue our development? We are all students in one form or another. We are all practicing. Practicing to become better at our crafts.

We often associate this with stereotyping and profiling. Stereotyping is synonymous with misrepresentation. This is why the title of this section, however, we often see profiling as a type of label that is most used by governmental and law enforcement entities. As with all things we come into contact with when we associate a label, there are always exceptions to the rule. Nothing can be written in stone when it relates to the tone of your skin or the philosophical nature of that human entity as if we are all truly each products of our environments then we would assume it safe to say profiling can sometimes also be a label wrongly attached.

During my elementary school years my parents always pushed reading on my sisters and me. We were always at a library, using the card catalog to look for books and topics of interest. There was no such thing as "google" or the Internet. You had to either go to a book store to read a physical book or you had to have a library card and go to a physical building called a library. One thing to note: Not all people in the library reading books wore glasses. So, you cannot say that reading books causes you to wear glasses. The more reading the more glasses is a falsity. Back then if you wore glasses you were called "four eyes" and were considered a "dork" or a "nerd". Time sure have changed as now the guy or gal with glasses is the scientist or the big money maker. Well, I guess it might have been back them to. Who wants to be a "dork" or a "nerd", well me if I can associate that term with money, right? I'll wear glasses if I can make more money.

Anyway, back to my story. I was in a class one day and the teacher was talking about animals and she was going around the room to each of us students and giving us a letter of the alphabet and asking us to name an animal starting with that letter. When it came to me she said "G". My letter was the letter "G". I immediately answered her with "Gnu". The teacher spoke up and said I was wrong. Everybody laughed at me and my response. I was a very shy kid and this didn't help matters either. She proceeded to ask me where I had heard such a thing and what kind of animal did I think I was talking about. I stood up and said the "Gnu, was a type of water buffalo in Africa." The teacher was shocked I had an answer. She went over to the row of books on the shelf, took out a book, and proceeded to read from the book. She was once again shocked I had known of an animal she had not heard of, and she was the teacher. The teacher who was supposed to be the all-knowing. Like I said, none of us know everything!

How about another example. I was a senior in high school and in an English class I had to compose a descriptive writing. I was to compose a writing describing one of my relatives. I chose to write about one of my uncles. In that writing I had a word in it "penchant". The teacher would take each of our writings and present them to the class. She would give our name, our composition title, then proceed to read them out loud. When it came to my turn, she gave my name, my title, then read the paper aloud. Then she said something about one of the words in my paper being out of place. The word was "penchant". She chastised me in front of everyone in the class for having my parents writing the paper for me! She asked me to stand up in class and explain why I used the word "penchant". I gave her an explicit explanation for the word "penchant". She never had me stand up in class again. I was right and she was wrong, although she never apologized.

One last thing, I will never forget. I was always rather good with the spelling of words. We would always be asked to spell words and lookup new words with our parents. I remember one word I was not sure of and will never forget. I was at a spelling bee. It was myself and one other students left standing. I was asked to spell, well, this might be difficult to get the point across. Let me give the definition first: "an organized group of singers or a choral group performing together". The word spelled correctly is "choir". I spelled it "quire". Like I said, nobody can now everything. I lost the spelling bee, but, I was one of the last ones standing! Counts for something, right?

# 4 ... STOP, LOOK, AND LISTEN

This chapter isn't about if you start something make sure you always finish it. It is about starting or becoming involved in something that might keep some part of your mental being or subconscious pulling you back in without even you realizing it is happening. Maybe you know better and start something anyway and you can't seem to stop doing it.

We hear of this thing called Karma. The thinking is that things we do or become involved in our past can come back in our future to either reward or deter us. Kind of makes sense, right? If you send that television evangelist $100 dollars and years later you receive $1000 dollars back, like he tells you, then it seems to work, right? If you don't send him the cash next month your television blows up, then you can blame him and or yourself for not sending the cold hard cask, right? Well, all joking aside. In my opinion, there are enough things in life that try and bring you down, so why do you need to assist them in your demise? Seems like common sense to me.

Other than this Karma thingy we have documentation starting at birth that follows along our trail of life that keeps track of, generally, the wrong things we do. I don't really know of any documented trail that follows us with all the positives we do, we just seem to keep track of that in our heads, then when we get into trouble we start detailing those positives in order that we may accentuate the positive and somehow override the current trouble. We've all done it, I am no exception to the rule.

The moral of this chapter is to not do something you may regret later. You probably know that it is wrong, but you say to yourself "just this once" and you think you can control it just by saying that. Like the potato chip commercial says "you can't eat just one". In general this rings true and you can research if you like.

## When I was young

I mentioned in another chapter of my stealing a belt buckle when I was a small kid. Well, later in life when I was in my teens I had another bout with that kind of life. I don't know what my problem was. Was it to get attention from my father? I don't really know. I truly have no idea. I could have been found guilty and put away for a time, and am surely glad I wasn't. I learned during this learning experience that jail was not the place for me in any stretch of my imagination. You really do see awful things and muffled screams day and night. Take my word, do all you can to prevent this type of situation and toe the line.

I had relatives in my family that were sheriffs, judges, jailers, and other law enforcement titles. That was the dream I had to be some kind of detective, Texas Ranger or the like. Well, after my prowess on the negative side of life and the documented record I had acquired there was no way for me to seek out a career in law enforcement. I myself ended those aspirations. I am not sure if that documentation ever goes away?

# Think First

Stop and think about what you might be thinking of doing. Look at the possible consequences of your actions as they are written somewhere in a policy. Listen to others who give you advice on those policies and the consequences. It is a form of prevention.

All human entities get into binds. All human entities have deadlines. All human entities get tired. If you dwell upon something over and over in your head you will try to justify and minimize. You will try to justify with reasons why you should or have to do something that is wrong. You will try to minimize the effect of what you are thinking of doing.

# No Matter What

There are many titles or terms we associate with theft: Plagiarism, Larceny, Burglary, Stealing, Robbery, and many others. They all stem from the same basis term theft. All these terms have different associations and different penalties and or ramifications according to their rank within our society. No matter what it is stealing, either physically or mentally stealing from another to hold and try to make or portray as your own.

Theft has always been around I would say since the beginning of time as we know it. There has always been someone who was envious of someone or something someone had and wanted what to gain it. Sometimes there are people who just don't want to take the time to do through the proper channels and ear it so they take the shortcut and steal it.

No matter what you call it! No matter how you justify it! No matter how you minimize it! It is stealing! It is not yours! And I promise you if you do it long enough and take enough changes and risks, you will pay a price for doing it.

# 5 ... PENCILS AND PAPER

Previous to the computer or cyber age there were two things called pencils and paper. Students took notes in all their classes from elementary school to post-secondary. If you planned on passing exams you took notes, rewrote those notes, studied those notes, and crammed those noted the night before an exam. You did all this if you wanted to pass that exam.

If you were writing an essay, researching a thesis, or compiling a dissertation you spent hours, weeks, and days going to libraries to read books. To use your pencil and paper to copy down references and citing's you thought were prevalent for your writing culmination. Some books were reference books and you could not check them out. Depending upon the type of paper you were writing or the method you may have to read and cite 20, 40, 60, or even several hundred books or articles. Highlights of each of these was written and rewritten and rewritten by you time and time over and over. This was the 100% physical gathering of information.

There were pros and cons to this type of gathering. The biggest pro is that through all this physical gathering, writing and rewriting, you are definitely the all-knowing when it comes to your topic. UNLESS. Are you listening? Unless you just skip all that work and copy the work of someone else and turn it in as your own. Back then there were no computers and no databases and no way of running someone's paper through a software program to see if it was their own work or plagiarized. Those things did not exist. In our day and time of today, yes, sometimes these papers are sometimes caught when they get digitized or technology is used to review them.

## Old Days Extended

I have compiled and written many papers, short and long, several thesis, multiple articles and two dissertations. I remember just a few of the ones I wrote during my high school tenure. The majority of papers I have written have been during my college and post-college years.

I started college in around 1994 and I remember the first post-education facility I went to had what was called a learning resource center (LRC). That LRC had five computers that were on some sort of network. That wasn't an internet network it was a network so we could type out our papers and print them instead of using an IBM selectric typewriter where you had to type each page and there was no such thing as memory. Memory was the notebook you physically wrote the paper in, then you attempted to type the paper out on a typewriter. If you wanted a copy you had to take your typed paper to the copier and make a copy.

We were lucky as we had a few computers where we could type out our paper then save our compilation on this black plastic 3.5 inch square called a floppy. This is where we could save our document. We also could print out one or more copies and did not have to take our first copy to the copier and make another one. This computer was a one-stop device. There were no labs and classrooms full of computers for students to use. Those did not exist at that time. A couple years later I transferred to another school and that school had computer laboratories. Laboratories of computers and students could go into them, do their work, and print in needed. The number one most amazing thing at that time in those computer labs was something called internet connectivity.

You could research virtually any topic that came to your mind. There were restrictions though. I remember I had to do an essay for an English class and I chose the John F Kennedy Assassination. That was my topic. I really myself was interested in this and all the conspiracy behind his death so I wanted to know more. However, that particular university had installed topic blocks they did not deem as appropriate for students to research. On that university campus when whenever I typed in anything even closely related to JFK, assassinations or the like a screen would pop up saying those topics was not available. I had to do all my research for my topic and at other public libraries who had computer access to the public or I had to find physical written books to read.

Over the next years of my AS, BS and first MS degree things and topics began to open up and be more available to us as students. That campus apparently decided those firewalled topics needed to be available as we were a university and those provisions needed to be available. Still during those degree years I spent taking notes in most all of my classes. I had learned by then that taking notes, writing notes, rewriting notes, and reading and cramming with those notes over and over again helped me to be successful to making the Dean's list every semester I was in school. This was important to me to have this high standing. Then if I ever thought of being caught at cheating or plagiarizing I knew how I would feel in front of my classmates and my professors to be known as the thief. That concept was not even in my scope of being. That was not acceptable for me. Integrity and honor was all I really had if you stripped away my façade. I would never jeopardize that.

## Then Later

During my years of my AS, BS and first MS we had computers and the internet. We could carry out somewhat limited research projects as we still had to go to physical libraries and look up physical books and resources. The difference was we used a laptop to copy and write our transitions to a hard disk and not a physical sheet of paper or spiral notebook. This were still quite limited as databases were limited as to what people had time to put things in them. You could not just type out a questions and get 600,000 answers to your query. The internet was still in a somewhat infancy.

Then as time went on the internet began to fill with answers, right and wrong. Pretty much the same as today. Real news and fake news.

Today we have copying and pasting directly from the internet and this new technology called Artificial Intelligence (AI). You can go to one of the AI programs and ask it to write you a five page essay on X and with 30 seconds it will type you up a five page essay on X. If you revert to this form of theft, be sure to check what you submit and make sure it is correct. Even if it is correct and you make few changes there are still software that will detect that your submission was written by AI.

Today you are more susceptible at being caught cheating and or plagiarizing. You may be able to run but you surely cannot hide. Once you get an infraction put on your student record it will follow you forever. It will follow you from school to school. Once you step in that cow pile the smell will follow you I promise you. Have you ever been in a field and stepped in a fresh cow pile? If so, you know what I mean.

The question is: Do you really want to get caught stealing and submitting something as your own. Is that all the integrity, honor and pride you have?

# 6 ... AS A STUDENT

A college degree isn't just a college degree for the sake of a fancy expensive paper to hang on your wall and impress your friends. The AS, BS, MS, and others are stepping stones. They are not one-stop shops of completion. The human element is never done learning. At least, industry doesn't see it that way. Industry sees you achieving those degrees as a means to gauge your motivation and prowess in attaining goals, setting new ones, and attaining those.

Companies want to know if they hire you, you have the motivation and drive to attain others they may set for you. This all depends upon the facility you become involved in or the area or field of your expertise. No one job title is the same at every location or within every industry. Generally there are a majority of similarities but never identical.

The last year of YOUR attempt at completing a university degree is the most critical! ALL years are critical, but generally the junior and senior years of a BS degree are when you come to certain realizations.

Yes, you may be involved in a straight BS degree in Cybersecurity. That will differ significantly with a BS in Computer Science with a track in Cybersecurity or Computer Information Security or similar. In a Computer Science specified program you will come into contact with additional courses in programming languages, discrete structures, higher level mathematics, and probably statistic related courses. The typical Cybersecurity degree pathway is more related to the Information Technology (IT) side of things. There are relationships with IT and CS but the CS side has a more difficult path to follow and achieve.

A Computer Science BS or MS degree is up there with the most difficult degrees as engineering. Programming languages, statistics, high level mathematics, and creative and critical problem solving are the reasoning behind this. If YOU look at other degrees YOU may find a few examples of some of these courses but all-in-all YOU generally will not. If YOU are in one of these programs YOU chose that program the program did not choose YOU! Expect some level of difficulty. If it was a simple and easy prospect the money for completion would not be as high as it is and neither would the positions be so available.

**Become Involved**

Become involved! This is in addition to YOUR normal course load. Look for projects within YOUR area of study. Talk to other students or professors to see what is available at the time. Each semester may offer different projects. Some of those projects may involve paid stipends. Some of those may involve travel internal and or external of the United States. This is all paid by grants, scholarships, or special funds. It won't cost YOU a penny but it is great experience to put on a resume. Employers look for these things.

How about an internship. It is up to YOU to seek out internships but sometimes professors within a department have links to these. If YOU do a great job for the intern employer they may offer YOU a position when YOU graduate. This happens quite often.

How about getting involved in competitions? These sometimes lead to job offers as well.

Put a resume together. Go to all recruiting events YOU see. Walk around and gather some business cards. Talk to some of the vendors. Ask them questions. That is why they came!

How about certifications or certificates? What are top ones in YOUR proposed area of expertise? Look up companies and see what they recommend for their employees and or applicants. Job advertisements can sometimes tell YOU a lot!

# Research

It would make sense for a student enrolled in a cyber security related program and taking a cyber security related course would start to think about things related to security and or cyber security. Right?

This is college, YOUR time going to k-12 classrooms is over. It is time to think like an adult and come to the realizations of an adult. Put YOUR cell phone down and pay attention!

Some employers look for degrees, some experience, some certificates, and some certifications. Some look for a combination of these.

Do a little searching, you know research. Look at some job advertisements. By now YOU should have an idea what area or specialty YOU see YOURSELF doing as a career.

Find 3 (Three) job advertisements within this state YOU may be interested in after YOU graduate. Answer the following questions for each of the 3.

1. Name of company
2. Brief description of company
3. Location or locations
4. Job title
5. Brief job description
6. Are they looking for: Degree, certifications, certificates, experience
7. Pay
8. Benefits
9. Does this company and or job posting look like something YOU might have interest in after graduation?
10. Would YOU be interested in an internship with this company, COOP, or OJT? Do they offer any of these?

The purpose of this assignment is to help to prepare YOU for YOUR future.

# Due Diligence

Have you ever heard the term "due diligence"? What exactly does that mean? It means simply, to do more than the bare minimum. Do more than just enough to get by and pass. Stand out from all the others. If you graduate and there are 100k other graduates competing for the same jobs what do you do? You must absolutely stand out from all the others! How do you stand out? By doing your due diligence.

## Up to You

In the end it all boils down to one thing. It is really all up to you! Success is up to you. Sometimes there external forces that seem to be preying upon your existence but it really is all up to you. If you try to ride the hose and fall off, it is up to you to get back on and try again. If it isn't you that makes the decision then who is it? Good things happen to bad people and bad things happen to good people. You can only justify and minimize things only so much, then they may turn on you. If something can go wrong it will.

Teachers, instructors, educators, professors, whatever you want to call them, they can only point at the doors. They can point at the doors and give you direction why you should choose that door if it opens. They cannot physically push you into a door you do not want to enter. You enter at your own risk. Are you prepared to enter that door? Sometimes we may enter a door and think we are prepared but fail. We have to get back up and try again. Sometimes, it might just not be the right door for us.

For many years I was an IT field technician and had a myriad of IT field techs working for my company. A lot of funny stories abound from all this driving.

One morning around dawn, I had been driving for several hours through the country. The sun was coming up. Up ahead I saw a bright blue plastic barrel, about a 30 gallon one, sitting on its side parallel with the ditch line beside the road. The closer I got I could see something behind the barrel. The closer I got I could see it was a wild hog. This was down in the south. Wild hogs roam free everywhere in the country. This rather large hog had his front legs up on the back of the barrel. He was grunting and snorting, having what seemed to be a rough time. He was on the back of this barrel trying to, what looked like, to push the barrel along the ditch line. I suppose he or she had a purpose in mind. I slowed down and stopped, next to the hog on the barrel, flipped up my sunglasses, rolled my window down, and looked at the hog. I asked what the hell he/she thought he/she was doing. I was laughing! This hog turned his head toward me and looked straight at me! This was for several minutes. He looked as if to say, "get your own barrel, this one is mine." I rolled up my window and drove off. On my return trip the barrel was still there in the same spot and the wild hog was gone.

The moral of that story is that hog wanted to move that barrel so much. No matter how hard he tried to move that barrel down the ditch line he could not move that barrel. He tried with all his might and all his being. It was just not meant to happen. It wasn't in the cards for that hog to move that barrel. If he had moved it what would he have done with it? Did he need or want a blur plastic barrel for a decoration for his mud pit? Maybe he would have gotten it home and his sow didn't think it matched the rest of the décor. What if? Life is full of what ifs.

Stay away from "what if" and try something. It is up to you to reach out and take hold of what you want. It is not up to the rest of the population if you fail. It isn't the population's fault fi you do not grab hold of the brass ring. It is up to you, only you can blame yourself. Life has plenty of excuses to go around.

# 7 ... SOFT AND HARD SKILLS

Anyway, what is a soft skill and what is a hard skill? A soft skill is generally a skill you might associate with the interaction between yourself and another human entity. A hard skill I associate with hard knowledge, maybe technical skills, you know tips and tricks you know related to the field you are in. Not things you THINK you know but things YOU know without a shadow of a doubt, realizations maybe?

Maybe you could call soft skills "people skills". You know: communication, teamwork, leadership, adaptability, and creativity. Then we have some more complex soft skills: networking, conflict resolve, time management, and problem solving. Soft skills often are complimentary to what I call the hard or technical skills. All industries look at these as skills they want their employees to possess. Some industries offer training of these skills they deem necessary in their employees once they are hired, but it is always a good idea to research around and do a review of what you possess and what you might need to work on.

**What are Employers looking for in an Employee?**

Certifications are NOT the only desirable qualities of an employee

Soft skills: *Soft skills* are the interpersonal attributes you need to succeed in the workplace. They are how you work with and relate to others—in other words, people skills.

- Communication
- Cooperation
- Ability
- Problem-solving ability
- Work ethics
- Social skills
- Time management
- Leadership
- Attention to details
- Critical thinking
- Self-confidence
- Handling pressure
- Decision making
- Negotiation
- Motivation
- Planning
- capability to Work Under Pressure
- Self-motivation
- Workplace conflict management
- Initiative work
- Flexibility to work
- Teamwork
- Imagination or vision

In CS, we have meetings with corporations each semester, and these are a few things employers are looking for. Sure, it is good to get a high GPA at graduation, but there are more aspects employers look for than a high GPA. They have said that a GPA is one of the last things they look at, that a high GPA is easily obtainable, that more things are needed other than that.

The more soft skills, you achieve, the better off you will be. You want to STICK out to the employers. You are competing with every other college and university in the world's graduates each semester. Make YOURSELF stand out from the rest.

If you feel you worked hard to complete the degree, why NOT go the extra steps to give that potential employer the "best choice candidate" to fill their position?

"Soft Skills" are the critical Key to winning that career position!

# 8 ... CERTIFICATES OR CERTICICATIONS

There are thousands of certificates and certifications. Why? There are thousands of companies that think you need to obtain them from them. If you are an IT field service technician you may work for a company that wants you to train for and obtain a certification or certificate on each device they send you to install, replace and or fix. This training may be online and or physical.

It is quite overwhelming the number of these that exist in the workplace. Most every company thinks you need some of these. Sometimes it is just a bargaining ploy when the company is trying to get a contract for a new venture. "All our technicians are BLANK certified". My honest advice being in industry for many years. Specially, if you are in your final years of a college degree. Do some research and look around at the type of company you may be looking at for a career. Research that company and see what certifications of certificates mean anything to them. Most companies in most all fields look at each other to see what their competition is doing. If you really look you will see they follow the same patters usually of what they are seeking in a specific employee.

There are public and private companies. There are careers in the public, private, government, military, etc. sectors. Get an idea of what they are looking for and strive to be that person. You want to be the graduate that sticks out from the rest. Don't get caught up In the hype do your research. Every company that offers certificates or certifications want you to get theirs, usually for a price. Do some browsing to see what others think of their offerings.

Certifications are MOST desirable along with Soft Skills

Something to keep in mind. Certifications have been around for many years. They are ever changing. New ones are popping up all the time. Some stay current and are updated, some fall to the wayside.

Whatever field you are seeking as a career? Look at certifications in that field. Not all fields accept the same ones. Just because your area is computer science, information technology, quality control, networking, security, etc. Does not mean they are all valid, either needed, wanted, or accepted.

If you are in the security area, then you need to seek out security certifications. Certificates of completion are NOT the same thing as certifications. You will see many companies and institutions offering certificates? This is sometimes misleading. A certificate says you have completed some type of training or some courses in a particular subject. It is NOT the same thing as taking a company made exam.

Example: Cisco is a networking company, if not the largest one, a very prevalent one. They offer many certification exams. These exams are developed and implemented by Cisco. There are companies and institutions that offer certificates related to their exams. The purpose of these certificates and or course offerings is to assist and PRIME a student, to take their exam.

To give them a foundation to get started learning the material for the exam. It is NOT, nor will that course or courses be the sole material the student will use when reviewing for the Cisco exam! Cisco offers their own training platforms, books, virtual environments, etc. You pay for these. Who better to study from than the exam maker themselves? You learn it their way.

## Years Ago

Not sure how many years ago? Vocational schools and technical schools were everywhere. It was decided they were not needed and the educational environments moved to community colleges (two year schools), to do the vocational/technical skills. There are still some vocational/technical schools, high school vocational wings, but MANY are gone now. That was a decision made then and it has come back to haunt the education of today, as skilled labor in the USA has suffered, as everyone wants a college four year education. So, some of these two year colleges offer certificates. If you are curious of a certificate? Contact the company that offers the certification and ask them of the validity of the certificate? You will soon find, these companies value the certification over the certificate.

Certifications are big business, big money. Some companies have developed week long seminars to prepare exam takers. These cost good money too.

"Don't spend money on something you think may help you, find out what WILL help you. Don't just take an exam because it is there. Most exams expire and have stipulations to keep them from expiring, like, another level exam."

Another example: CompTIA is a company and all they do is create exams for their generic certifications. They offer MANY exams. "I think around 30 or so years ago they got involved with some computer hardware/software companies and offered training certifications." This began to take off. They contacted the US military and government and said their training would be a good for their employees, as this training would be a baseline or foundation for trainable employees.

## Currently

Well, the US believed it. Here we are today, CompTIA has a certification for MANY things. Some you have heard of are the: A+, Network+, and Security+. "If you seek a job in the US government or military as a contractor, they will ask if you have TWO of these three, hands down! If not, they will not keep your resume, they believe you need these to work for them, as a starting point. Now, the bad: The A+ was the first exam certification they offered. If you took the exam (hardware/software combined) you kept the cert forever, it never expired! Several years later, CompTIA saw the money to be made and now the certs last for three years. Now the A+ is actually two exams, a hardware and a software exam. They can be split into two, but they still may offer them together, I am not sure? I got mine years ago, and got very high scores. I missed one question on each exam.

Every three years, you either take the new version of the exam, or you take another CompTIA exam and YOU will keep whatever exams you hold as current. Every two years prepare to take another CompTIA exam to keep their certs you have. (Each version of a CompTIA exam changes every year or two). Each exam is like a few hundred bucks. If a company you work for deems certain exams are relevant to their employees, they will usually pay for employees to get them. Several hundred dollars each, usually.

Anyway, this is my story and I'm sticking to it.

# 9 ... PREPPING, GETTING, AND KEEPING

There are a lot of things we take for granted. We sometimes think we know the answer, but do we really? Maybe someone else has the correct answer? "It is what it is" isn't applicable to everything on the earth. Each person can sway his/her destiny if they choose? Generally! There are ALWAYS exceptions to the "every rule".

Ask yourself: Is there anything I can do to help my chances? Could I have done more? When you are young, you have a better chance to give yourself better chances!

There are additions to this list, this is just from the top of my head.

## Preparing ...

- Go to class on time.
- Cleanliness.
- When someone is talking, listen.
- Put the cell phone down – "You are NOT on a game show and need a lifeline".
- Never tell your professor that you only want to complete the points necessary to pass the class. Really?
- Dress really isn't an issue in school generally, but, for some professors/instructors it is?

Professors/instructors get calls all the time about potential candidates or are asked if they have any outstanding presentable students.
- Get involved in activities, clubs, and organizations. You never know who you will come in contact with.
- Certificates. There are free ones if you do some research. Even take some exams in your field and get some certifications.
- It is a WHO you KNOW world and will ALWAYS be.
- If you don't know, ask. Don't just take something for granted, that it is as it seems.
- Put a resume together early. There are a lot of career fairs. Go to them! You never know who you might meet? They may have internships/scholarships?
- Google internships/scholarships.

## Getting ...

- First impression – Firm handshake.
- Get a haircut and take a bath?
- Dress to impress – Also a first impression. Dress for the position you are trying to get. (You don't wear a three piece suit to a gardener job, and you don't wear gold chains and a tee shirt to an engineer position)
- If you apply to a company, do a little research. (What do they do? How large? Employees?)
- No interviewer likes anything better than to see you took the time to have researched his/her company. During the interview ask them a few questions about the company.

- Don't lie about what you know or can do. If you don't know say you don't but are willing to learn.
- Have a nice layout for a resume and cover letter. (Be brief but hit the high points. Relate the resume to the position requirements. If multiple positions, tailor each resume to each position. ONE resume/cover letter does NOT fit all.)
- Be ready for a drug test – (Trust me, you never know. If you are a great fit for the job on the first interview, you may be asked to complete this? Are you willing to lose a good job for something childish? "When I was a child, I talked like a child, I thought like a child, I reasoned like a child. When I became a man, I set aside childish ways.")
- After the interview. Send a THANK YOU letter! Quickly! The next day. A letter is MORE personal than an e-mail. Remember, you took the TIME to write the letter and send it, the interviewer KNOWS this too. It keeps YOU on the mind of the interviewer.

## K e e p i n g ...

- Haircut and bath? You are NOT going to the beach, or are you?
- What is everyone else wearing? (Not the single rebel that stands out).
- Get involved.
- Can you get company paid education, certifications? If so, get them. Make yourself valuable.

- Keep your resume updated – You never know when you will need it.
- Be ready for the drug test.

# 10 ... SUCCESS IS UP TO YOU

In the end it all boils down to one thing. It is really all up to you! Success is up to you. Sometimes there external forces that seem to be preying upon your existence but it really is all up to you. If you try to ride the hose and fall off, it is up to you to get back on and try again. If it isn't you that makes the decision then who is it? Good things happen to bad people and bad things happen to good people. You can only justify and minimize things only so much, then they may turn on you. If something can go wrong it will.

Teachers, instructors, educators, professors, whatever you want to call them, they can only point at the doors. They can point at the doors and give you direction why you should choose that door if it opens. They cannot physically push you into a door you do not want to enter. You enter at your own risk. Are you prepared to enter that door? Sometimes we may enter a door and think we are prepared but fail. We have to get back up and try again. Sometimes, it might just not be the right door for us.

For many years I was an IT field technician and had a myriad of IT field techs working for my company. A lot of funny stories abound from all this driving.

One morning around dawn, I had been driving for several hours through the country. The sun was coming up. Up ahead I saw a bright blue plastic barrel, about a 30 gallon one, sitting on its side parallel with the ditch line beside the road. The closer I got I could see something behind the barrel. The closer I got I could see it was a wild hog. This was down in the south. Wild hogs roam free everywhere in the country. This rather large hog had his front legs up on the back of the barrel. He was grunting and snorting, having what seemed to be a rough time. He was on the back of this barrel trying to, what looked like, to push the barrel along the ditch line. I suppose he or she had a purpose in mind. I slowed down and stopped, next to the hog on the barrel, flipped up my sunglasses, rolled my window down, and looked at the hog. I asked what the hell he/she thought he/she was doing. I was laughing! This hog turned his head toward me and looked straight at me! This was for several minutes. He looked as if to say, "get your own barrel, this one is mine." I rolled up my window and drove off. On my return trip the barrel was still there in the same spot and the wild hog was gone.

The moral of that story is that hog wanted to move that barrel so much. No matter how hard he tried to move that barrel down the ditch line he could not move that barrel. He tried with all his might and all his being. It was just not meant to happen. It wasn't in the cards for that hog to move that barrel. If he had moved it what would he have done with it? Did he need or want a blur plastic barrel for a decoration for his mud pit? Maybe he would have gotten it home and his sow didn't think it matched the rest of the décor. What if? Life is full of what ifs.

Stay away from "what if" and try something. It is up to you to reach out and take hold of what you want. It is not up to the rest of the population if you fail. It isn't the population's fault fi you do not grab hold of the brass ring. It is up to you, only you can blame yourself. Life has plenty of excuses to go around.

# 11 ... MY CYBERSECURITY COURSE ACTIVITIES

In all of my courses I have activities I specifically make for student s to actually think and to find ways to try and relate something physically and or mentally to the student relative to the course topic.

These activities may involve discussions, oral and or PowerPoint presentations, short or long essays, and what I call thinking assignments which are answered in a few short paragraphs.

## Discussions

These are made for students to give their ideas and or opinions on certain topics. Once they give their opinion other students will then join their discussion.

## Oral/PowerPoints

Students will be asked to research and put together a PowerPoint presentation. A presentation which may be given orally to the class if semester time permits.

## Thinking Assignments

I generally give students a scenario and ask them how they might resolve that scenario or give their opinion as to how to resolve.

## Essays

These entail a little more research than the previous assignments. Here again I try to make the students think and support their thoughts with references from the field.

This course YOU are in this semester is related to cyber security. So, it would make sense for a student enrolled in a cyber security related program and taking a cyber security related course would start to think about things related to security and or cyber security. Right?

This is college, YOUR time going to k-12 classrooms is over. It is time to think like an adult and come to the realizations of an adult. Put YOUR cell phone down and pay attention!

## Random Topics

These are topics I have put together that I have found through my years to be relevant of run parallel with thought related to security, information technology and or network engineering. These topics can be the primer for any of the activities I have mentioned above.

### Feeling Safe

How safe do YOU feel? Do YOU feel secure when YOU go home and lock the door? Do YOU feel safe when YOU are in a classroom? Do YOU feel safe when YOU go downtown in the city and walk into a department or restaurant? Do YOU notice the safety precautions around YOU? Do YOU notice where the entrances and safety exits are if a situation erupts or breaks out? What do YOU do in a building YOU have never been into before if a fire breaks out? Do YOU propose to just randomly trample over other men, women, and children to get out, so YOU can be saved?

THESE THINGS HAPPEN EVERYDAY! ARE YOU PREPARED?

Let me slim this topic down a bit!

Do YOU feel safe at home? Are there locks on all outside doors? What type of locks? Are they electronic, mortise, smart, deadbolt, keyless, magnetic, disc, barrel, etc. Do YOU know what type they are? Do YOU know how safe they are? Do YOU know how easy or how hard they are to break or get past?

How about each outward facing door? What is the door made of? Is it made of wood, plastic, fiberglass, composite, glass, etc.? Have YOU ever payed attention to that? Could that door be easily kicked in or shattered?

How about the windows? How are they locked? Are YOU safe inside a security system?

THINK ABOUT IT!

Think about these things at all the buildings YOU go into each day, the classrooms, the restaurants, the department stores, etc.

Example: No example here, let's get right to the activity!

YOU do understand that invasions happen every day, right? What is an invasion? An invasion is when one or more human entities gather together, generally with criminal intent, to invade the space of other human entities through force! Home invasions is just one of those derivatives! Home invasions are typically carried out by two populations: Invaders who know their victims and invaders who do not! Just to clarify, forensically, any could have some unseen or unnoticed relationships.

This happens every day!

Invaders may just walk in through an open door, then lock it behind them. Invaders could kick down the door and take hostages. Invaders could pick a simple door lock and just walk right in. Invaders could keep it quiet and use a glass cutter to gain entrance.

The truth is: If someone really wants to get to YOU they will! It might take the right time and circumstance, but they will if they are patient and wait! The ting about security is: There is NO such thing as 100% security! It does not exist! YOU will learn that during these security related courses and program!

Here is YOUR activity................

Look at the past page YOU have read here. Think about YOUR house, apartment, dorm room, etc. Think about where YOU live. Think about where YOU lay and rest YOUR head at night. Is it safe? Do YOU feel safe?

Doors, locks, windows, etc.

On ONE hand: What if someone or others were trying to get to YOU? How hard would it be to get in through windows, doors, etc.? Think about what we have been talking about.

On the OTHER hand: What if something happened and YOU need to get out? What if YOU are hurt and do not have access to all of YOUR mental and or physical faculties?

The purpose of this assignment is to be aware of YOUR surroundings, specifically, where YOU live. Where YOU say YOU feel safe. Are YOU really safe? After looking at these things through a new lens do YOU still feel the same? Do YOU have any plans to change something YOU have found that has made YOU aware?

## A w a r e n e s s

When YOU go somewhere are YOU aware? Are YOU aware of what is going on in the background or foreground around YOU? Are YOU paying attention?

Example: I do not know how many times I have been walking and some human entity is on the same sidewalk heading toward me and looking at their cell phone and NOT paying attention to what is going on around them! They expect everyone around them to be aware of them and move out of their path. I don't know how many times I moved out of their way and they didn't even look up to see who or what I was!

Here are my questions: Do YOU realize the shape of the world today when it relates to crime? Do YOU realize someone could do YOU harm and YOU not even see who was involved? These are just a couple of questions off the top of my head. I could write over 100 questions related to this topic, awareness!

Children get kidnapped every day because parents were not pay attention. People get assaulted, kidnapped, raped, and or murdered every day and nobody sees anything, remembers anything, or can describe anything. Don't YOU think YOU have a certain responsibility? If not for YOURself….for others? YOU may NOT be in total control of the situation, BUT, YOU might be able to help! Would YOU want someone to stand up and help YOU?

THINK ABOUT IT!

FYI

Some stores have security people, loss prevention people, store detectives, etc. These people are aware of YOU! YOU may not see them watching YOU but in some stores they are! Some store even have cameras at their entrances! They take the photo of every human entity that goes through their doors and puts that photo into a database. After the facial photo is taken facial recognition software then looks through the database and sees if there is a match. If at any point there is a match, and that human entity was banned from shopping at that store then security personnel are notified and that human entity will be found within the store and escorted out.

YOU can bet money that employees in the store are aware of YOU even if YOU do not see them!

Here is YOUR activity................

Take a couple of hours and go somewhere. It can be a department store, a restaurant, a park, pretty much anywhere. Pick a place. Leave YOUR phone in the car or leave it in YOUR pocket! """If YOU really want to understand this activity? Go somewhere where YOU stick out! Where YOU are NOT the normal look of the human entity that goes there."""

Pay attention to what is going on in that facility.

On ONE hand..........Do YOU notice anyone paying attention to YOU? Has one of their employees spoken to YOU and or acknowledged YOUR presence? Does it seem as though someone is following YOU around or watching YOU? How are YOU dressed? Do YOU look like YOU belong there or not?

On the OTHER hand........Do YOU see anyone out of place? Do YOU see anyone that looks like they do not belong there? Do YOU see anyone that makes YOU feel uneasy?

The purpose of this assignment is to be aware of YOUR surroundings! When crime happens, law enforcement people come to the scene and ask this: Did YOU see anything? What did YOU see? YOU can bet that a law enforcement student can go into that facility, come out and write a five page report on what he/she saw. What is the difference in YOU either being a law enforcement student and or a cyber security student? Both of these students are involved in the prevention, maintenance, and forensics of security.

## Car-Jacking

Car-Jacking happens every day! What is car-jacking? Car-jacking is when one or more human entities (criminals) actively remove the driver and or passengers from a vehicle and drive off.

Are YOU prepared? YOU never know, right?

Example: No example here, let's get right to the activity!

YOU do understand that car-jacking happen every day, right?

Here is YOUR activity................

"If by chance YOU have a self-defense weapon in YOUR vehicle don't think for a minute they don't have an offensive weapon to either act or counter-act against YOUR weapon."

What if YOU were driving in YOUR car alone and YOU came up to a stop light. It was late at night. Someone came up to YOUR car door and pointed a gun at YOU and said to open the door! YOU opened the door, they got in. They drove YOU a few blocks and threw YOU out of the car into the street while the car was moving.

What would be YOUR detailed plan of action for the next 24 hours? How do YOU think YOU would feel?

What do YOU think YOU would do? Who would YOU tell? Who would YOU call? How would YOU prepare for the next time, or the first time?

## Drugging

Drugging's happen every day! What is a Drugging? A drugging is when one or more human entities (criminals) covertly sneak a drug into the drink of an unsuspecting victim or victims to possess one or more possessions they deem wanted or needed. Sometimes the victim or victims survive and sometimes they do not!

Are YOU prepared? YOU never know, right?

Example: About three years ago. One of my best friends had a son, he was 30 years old, an outgoing person, and the kind of person who never knew a stranger. He could and would have been friends with anyone! He was out of town working with his dad for several months doing outdoor contract work. One weekend he came to his dad and said after work that day he was going to drive out to San Francisco. It was only three hours away so it was not a real long trip. His dad said fine, YOU are an adult and I'll see YOU when YOU get back.

This son called his parents every day or night. A day went by and no call. A second day went by and no call. The parents called the local police and mentioned they had not heard from their son and it was unlike him to not call for one day let alone two days. The police did a GPS check with the son's cell phone provider. The police went to the GPS location and it was a hotel room downtown. The police knocked on the door and there was no answer. The police found the hotel manager and got him to open the door with a pass key.

My friend's son was laying on the bed fully dressed, the TV was on. It was like he had just laid down on the bed to watch TV and fell asleep. The problem was he was dead! There was NO sign of struggle. He had his wallet in his back pocket and all his credit cards were there. There was NO cash in his wallet.

The autopsy discovered there was a drug in his system. A drug that some people give to others to make them pass out. A RAPE drug is what it is called. It is called that but criminals also use it to rob unsuspecting victims. Sometimes the victims wake up and sometimes they are overdosed and do not wake up. Well, in this case he did not wake up!

YOU do understand that this happens every day, right?

Here is YOUR activity................

What if this was YOU? What if YOU woke up? Maybe 24 or 48 hours later?

Maybe YOU like doing things alone. Maybe YOU are more trusting of people than YOU should be? What if YOU are just not a very cautious person and YOU take it for granted that most people are good and only want to help? YOU do not have to be in a bar situation to get drugged. Maybe YOU have never had an alcoholic drink, so, any form of liquid can be tainted with a drug!

What would be YOUR detailed plan of action for the next 24 hours? How do YOU think YOU would feel? What do YOU think YOU would do? Who would YOU tell? Who would YOU call? How would YOU prepare for the next time, or the first time?

### R e g r e t s

Have YOU ever known anyone that did something they should have not done? Maybe something that they may have regretted doing? All human entities have a past and most have a future. We all do stupid things in our lives. Some of us live to tell about them. Some of us could write a book about them as we have done so many, too many to list here. I can say for certain that I have and I should probably not be alive today. I always say I have nine lives.

Example: When I was about 2 years old. I went to the store with my mother. I saw this shiny object hanging on a hook. It was unusual to me. I put the item in my pocket. When I got home I pulled out the item and started playing with it. My mother asked me where I got it and I said at the store. She immediately took me back to the store and made me hand it to the clear, tell him what I had done, and apologize. Of course, corporal punishment was enlisted at my house, so I got a spanking I am sure. I would guess the spanking made me regret what I had done?

Have YOU ever done something YOU should have not done? If YOUR plan is to become involved in a security related career, make it a point, NOT to mess up those chances by doing something YOU may regret later that might keep YOU from YOUR goal! If YOU get a negative record with a law enforcement agency it alone may hinder YOUR intentions!

THINK ABOUT IT!

Human entities do things every day they regret. Some human entities more than others. The thing about tit is: If YOU do not start it in the first place YOU won't have to worry about it! If YOU do not steal a first time then YOU will not have to worry about it a second time! If YOU do not cheat the first time then YOU will not be worried about being caught! Some time's we do things we justify and minimize in our mind. We know it is wrong and we try it anyway. Maybe we get away with it? Sometimes our minds come back to haunt us and just can't let some things go. The lesson is: If YOU don't try it in the beginning then YOU do not have to worry about it!

Example: I have quite a few regrets. One I have quite often. My dad died several years ago. We were never really close. He was a staunch disciplinarian. He was a military man. He was big and strong. I came into contact with his belt more times than I care to remember. I was not a good kid by any means. I guess I wanted more attention? My dad was always working. He never took me to a sports game. We never passed a ball around in the yard. Dad was always working and mom was the homemaker. Dad would go work in another state for months or years and return home with presents for us kids or we would follow him to the new state after a time. We moved 27 times before my senior year of high school. Anyway, I never realized when I was Younger why he was the way he was, why he was never around, etc. I didn't realize until I got older! Some things I just did not realize until after his death, why he was the way he was. When WE both got older I never really went out of my way to befriend him and at least let my guard down and try. This still bothers me to this day. Maybe I could have reached out and done something? I blame myself for part of that!

Here is YOUR activity................

Think about what YOU have just read. There is no right or wrong answer here. No one on the planet is perfect. Everyone has a past and has done something we can look back on and say we should have not done that! YOU do not have to be specific, just think about how YOU want to answer this activity. If YOU have no specific issue to spell out then maybe someone YOU know has?

## S t r u g g l e s

There is a saying that has been around for many years. I am not sure where it came from but I have heard it all my life. "What doesn't kill YOU makes YOU stronger."

In life, it is a fact that, human entities are born with no knowledge, a blank slate. Our brains are empty. We have never been able to use our senses to gain knowledge which then would transfer to our brains and therefore, learn. YOU cannot learn from experiences unless YOU have them! YOU cannot gain positive experiences unless YOU come into contact with them, and vice-versa for negative experiences.

Another saying: "We are products of our environments." From the day we are born, human entities come out into the world seeking interaction. If YOU have ever been around a little child, it seems the only word they know is "Why"? Why, Why, Why, Why, and Why? It seems it is a never-ending question.

Every situation we come in contact with during our lives on this planet we gain knowledge. We really don't realize most of the time, but our brain is working 24/7 to process information our senses give it. This happens from when we awake for our day, until we go to bed, and during our naps and sleep. Some of our thoughts and processes are slower and some of ours are faster. Whether YOU realize it or not YOU are a product of YOUR environment. YOU are a product of everything YOU have come into contact with since the day YOU were born.

THINK ABOUT IT!

Example: YOU are a product of everything YOU have come into contact with since the day YOU were born. We all have positive and negative things that happen in our lives. Positives generally build us up and negatives tend to tear us down. Positives give us motivation and negatives give us question. Another saying I have heard my whole life: "Bad things happen to good people and good things happen to bad people." It is relatively a never ending cycle human entities go through each day. Sometimes new things happen and sometimes they repeat. Some good and some bad.

There is no such thing as perfection. If there was, we would have good happen all the time. This isn't realistic. YOU have to accept the good with the bad.

Here is YOUR activity……………

Motivation can come in many forms…Struggles happen to all of us. PICK ONE thing, either positive or negative, that has happened during YOUR life that has motivated YOU to seek an education. In addition, add answers to these questions:

What motivated you?
How will that motivation keep YOU on track?

The purpose of this assignment is to be aware of YOUR motivation! To keep YOUR motivation! To not let anything remove YOUR motivation! Motivation is success! YOU want to achieve success, right?

### A s s a u l t i n g

Assaults and muggings happen every day! What is an assault or a mugging? An assault or mugging is when one or more human entities (criminals) actively attack one human entity or multiple human entities to possess one or more possessions they deem wanted or needed. Sometimes the victim or victims put up a fight, sometimes the victims survive and sometimes they do not!

Are YOU prepared? YOU never know, right?

Example: When I was little I was small for my age and I really didn't start to grow bigger until I was in junior high school. I was bullied when I was little by the playground bully, and I think he helped to make me what I am today, because of it. I guess. When I got older I got involved in PKA competitions and Karate. I hold a master belt in Tae Kwon Do and have quite a few trophies. I cannot say I am the consummate hero but after growing up and attaining knowledge and skills I can say I am not really afraid of anything or anyone on this planet, since I was say 16 years old. I am now 60 and still not afraid of anyone or anything, but I do realize, life is not fair, and sometimes things happen we have no control over.

Now to my story. I was with several friends on River Street in Savannah Georgia. We were walking around, drinking and partying, just having a big time. There were four of us. Two girls and two guys. "I have always had this sense about me, like a little man on my shoulder, a little man that keeps me out of trouble and makes me aware of things. Things that may happen or are about to. Kind of like a premonition. A mental guess that often turns out to be right!" In this case I think my little man was looking out for me! Years ago I carried a wallet in my back pocket that was long. A cowboy wallet, if YOU know what that is? Dollar bills go in it lengthwise and YOU don't have to fold them. This type of wallet does not just go down out of sight in YOUR back pocket, it sticks out, above the pocket. It is really an easy wallet to steal if YOU are in a large crowd of people.

Anyway, my wallet was in my back pocket. I felt the presence of someone staring at me. I glanced around and there was a group of five or six YOUng guys watching me and my friends. I noticed they were trying to play it off when they spoke to each other but I could see they were looking at my wallet. They kept looking at my wallet and talking to each other. This went on for about twenty minutes. It seemed as though they were following us. I took the wallet from my back pocket and put it into one of my front pockets and the group of YOUng guys shortly after seemed to disappear. I guess YOU could say I thwarted or upset their plans of a potential theft.

YOU do understand that this happens every day, right?

Here is YOUR activity................

What if YOU were alone, walked down a dark side street and got knocked on the head and were out for a time laying alone in an alley and then woke up? What would be YOUR detailed plan of action for the next 24 hours? How do YOU think YOU would feel? What do YOU think YOU would do? Who would YOU tell? Who would YOU call? How would YOU prepare for the next time, or the first time?

### Leader

Are YOU a leader or a follower? Just because YOU might think YOU are one or the other does not mean YOU actually are. YOU may see YOURSELF as one but in fact YOU are the other in reality. How do others see YOU? How do YOU see others?

Leaders never have an excuse, followers always have an excuse. Followers justify and minimize, leaders do not. Leaders know what they have to do, plan to do it, and carry it out. Leaders are generally managers or at least can or could be managers. Followers think they know where and how to be in that management role but often do not succeed or are quickly found out and removed.

Leaders generally stay leaders, followers can become leaders, leaders can become followers, and generally followers will always be followers.

YOU are YOUR guide and conductor through YOUR life! There is NO book to buy to guide YOU! Life is all trial and error! YOU learn from YOUR mistakes, hopefully, or maybe you do not. Leaders learn from their mistakes and followers generally keep making the same ones over and over and over and continue with the excuses as to why they could not do something or get something completed.

There are also labels of introverts and extroverts. Introverts are behind the scenes human entities and extroverts like it out in the limelight. Just because YOU are an introvert does not mean YOU cannot be a leader! Just because YOU are in extrovert does not mean YOU are a true leader. Internal and external personalities play no part for delineation when situations arise. Something drastic may happen in your life that brings YOU out of your follower shell to bring you to leader label. Then the same may be true of a leader, something drastic can push you into a follower shell if the situation pushes hard enough to overcome that barrier.

Example: When I was in my early 20s I took a job at a Lowes store. I started out working in the Lawn and Garden Center loading customer vehicles. After the season was over I was moved up to the manager position of the Plumbing department. The department was a mess and the previous manager had not been taking care of the department. He wasn't taking care of the workers nor the ordering of merchandise to fill the shelves. In a month I had the department working like a well-oiled machine. After a couple of months I was moved to the manager position in the Electronics department. I shortly got it in order and was moved to Electricity. After fixing that department I was moved as the manager of Paint. I got that department in order shortly. Within six months I was a zone manager in that store. Back then, Lowes had a magazine they printed out several times a year telling about employees and special things within the company. That year my progress up the ladder within Lowes made an article in that magazine. I was the first employee in Lowes history to move up so fast from the very bottom to a higher lever within management. This is just one single position in which I proved myself and there have been many others.

Here is YOUR activity................

Are YOU a leader or a follower? Do YOU think YOU are a leader or a follower? Write up a story providing proof if YOU are a leader. This is just not asking if YOU think YOU are a leader, YOU must provide at least one example.

The purpose of this assignment is to see:

Are YOU a leader?

Do YOU think YOU are a leader? Why, if YOU do not have proof?

Sometimes we are wrong in our thinking……

## Profiling

Do you understand what "Profiling" is?

Profiling is kind of like a bulleted description or sketch. Profiling is a prolific or creative form of labeling. Labeling with an exhaustive list of traits. We see a lot these days on TV and the news about profiling. If YOU do some research YOU will see that pretty much all law enforcement entities use profiling to catch the bad guy. The FBI, CIA, DHS, NCI, and ATF are some of these entities. Some human entities spend years of their lives learning how to profile and how the examine proofs to put together profiles. Profiling saves lives. I'm not going to reach out here and give an opinion as to whether or not the pros of profiling far outweigh the cons. This isn't my place. The reason I write these assignments is for YOU to review and give YOUR opinions.

Social media is much more prominent in our current times than it was 20/30 years ago. It is in-your-face and available everywhere. YOU see things presented and published today that would not have even been a thought or available back then. Good or bad it is here!

I do, however, think sometimes law enforcement gets a bad wrap/rap overall. Yes, I will agree there are bad apples around many corners, but I think YOU cannot blame all of law enforcement for the issues with some of them.

Have YOU ever watched a TV show called Andy Griffith, from the 1960s? This was a popular show that came on each week about a small town Sheriff, his deputy and his family. It must have been popular it was on for eight years, and is still on some TV channels today. Then there was another show that ran from 1968 to 1975 called Adam-12. A show about two Police officers in a Metro City environment.

I graduated high school in 1982. During the next ten or so years I got to know quite a few Police officers. Several of the guys I went to elementary, junior and high school became Police officers. If any of YOU are old enough to remember back during those times every Police car in the US had a sticker on it. That sticker said "To Serve and To Protect." If YOU can remember that far back? That was the thinking of the law enforcement personnel at that time. As a matter of fact, when I was younger in a small town, if myself and or my buddies were out doing something we should not be doing, the local police would follow us home or take us home. They would tell us to stay home and they did not want to see us back out again tonight!

What changed? What changed in the mentality of the law enforcement personnel? Why did, all of a sudden, we not see the sticker on vehicles anymore? What changed this? I'll tell YOU what changed the way of thinking that had been so prominent for all of law enforcement. The thinking that law enforcement was there to be helping hand to the people. War is what happened!

When wars end what happens to the military participants? Most of the ones who are not killed or wounded come back to their old towns looking for work. Also, since crime goes up every year and never seems to go down there are always available law enforcement positions open and available. For a person who has spent years and or multiple deployments providing security and or a form of law enforcement throughout the world, where do YOU think they might be applicable to find a position or job? That's right, the law enforcement sector. Some local law enforcement personnel might wear the old school beige/brown uniforms but most of the time YOU see tactical gear and BDUs (Battle Dress Uniforms) either camouflage or solid colors. That didn't happen by accident.

The dress (uniform) brings the mentality and or the mentality defines the dress. That is what happened! To serve and protect changed!

THINK...........................

This course YOU are in this semester is related to cyber security. So, it would make sense for a student enrolled in a cyber security related program and taking a cyber security related course would start to think about things related to security and or cyber security. Right?

This is college, YOUR time going to k-12 classrooms is over. It is time to think like an adult and come to the realizations of an adult. Put YOUR cell phone down and pay attention!

Example: When you think about law enforcement. YOU do not think about prevention YOU think about after-the-fact. The only time most people deal with Police officers is when something has happened, after-the-fact. They are sometimes involved in prevention activities, but most of the time we associate them with criminals. After all, during the daily routine of the typical law enforcement entity the majority of the people they deal with are questionable and or criminal people. So, what do we expect? If YOU deal with those types of people all day every day then I would assume they might expect everyone to be a questionable or criminal element when they come into contact with them. I would assume.

Here is YOUR activity................

What do you think about profiling? Prove any thoughts you have on this topic. If YOU pick the Pro side YOU must also have proof from the Con side and vice-versa. I do NOT want just an idea or thought YOU have I want you to give a legitimate debate.

The purpose of this assignment is to open your eyes to the idea of profiling.

# Assassination

Security...........................

"There is NO such thing as 100% security! It does not exist. It is only an idea."

This past weekend one of the US Presidential candidates had a rally. The rally was outside on a farm in Pennsylvania. Outdoors in the summer heat of July. There was an assassination attempt upon the Presidential candidate, previous President Donald Trump.

I was watching the TV announcement minutes after the attempt, when the special bulleting came across all channels on the TV. I saw the Presidential candidate on the stage speaking, he turned his head to his right, he pulled his hand up to the side of his head then he dropped to the ground. Then he was swarmed by Secret Service agents until they raised him up and led him to his vehicle and was driven off.

At that moment in time on the TV screen they had not advertised the assassination attempt but I could clearly see he had defied death. If at that precise moment if the past President had not turned his head to the right side he would be dead at this time. He would have been pronounced deceased at that time on the stage. I hope he realizes how he cheated death. Later that might all the news channel are talking about the assassination attempt. Matter of fact: Mr. Trump was the first to release a statement that it was actually a bullet that grazed his ear. Not the authorities, or the press, Mr. Trump was the first to release that!

There have been other assassination attempts on US Presidents in our past. We never had the social media back then we have today. Today everyone has a cell phone with a camera in their hand or their pocket. It is hard to escape the news. News today can really travel before the news people get it! This is good in some aspects and in others not so good. Before everyone had a cell phone in their pocket law enforcement would be able to suppress information until facts were attained and or investigations were started until releasing information to the press and therefore to the civilian population. Not, there is no suppression! Fake news, false news, and everyone has an opinion and wants to give it! The media really promotes this.

At that event, the bullet grazed the ear of Mr. Trump but kept going. The bullet has to go somewhere. Apparently, there were other bullets as well as one on the event attendees was shot and killed as well as several wounded by bullets. Just the mere attendance of events like these pose a threat to anyone that attends. The people wounded or killed had no idea when they got up that morning of the later day events. They were just going out to express their opinions and display their rights.

Back to what I said earlier. "There is NO such thing as 100% security! It does not exist. It is only an idea."

MY question: How did the shooter get so close to the candidate to allow him to expel several rounds at the candidate and crowd? I think it was around 130 or so years away. A football field is 100 yards if that gives you some perspective of the distance away. How does someone get that close? I'll tell you how: Failure. Complacency. Laziness. You think it will not happen to you, until it does! This is basically the answer. YOU or your team become so…Well…You let your guard down! Then it happens! Have you ever heard the saying: "If something can go wrong it will?" Well, this is the answer! If YOU leave something open to chance, chance has a way of getting in!

You are in security! Learning security! Keeping computers safe from a virus, you have to keep your guard up and install software and keep it updated. Keeping a network safe, you have to keep your guard up and install hardware and software and keep it patched and updated. Nothing is 100% safe and secure BUT you keep it as safe and secure as you can with the knowledge and money you have.

THINK……………..

Do a little research about past assassination attempts? They can be on anyone. Choose anyone single one or multiple ones.

Look at the attempts that FAILED or were SUCCESSFUL. DO NOT DO JFK! That has been beaten to death!

The purpose of this assignment is to be secure!

Tell myself and the class what you think? How was the attempt carried out? Who on who? What happened? How were they able to get so close? Did this attempt cause anything to change? Did anyone/we learn anything from it?

# Eminent Domain

Quite a few years back one of my roommates after college mentioned he wanted to invest in some real estate. It was several years after my flight school years and he was already a successful pilot for a major airline. He made quite a large amount of money and wanted to invest. As he was an airline pilot, he had traveled throughout all the territories owned by the United States.

He was interested in Puerto Rico as it was a United States Territory and Costa Rica, but Costa Rico was not a territory of the USA.

My friend mentioned at that time there were many investment opportunities in those areas off the Caribbean Ocean. He talked about how beautiful the beaches, the coastline, waterfalls, cliffs, etc.

He said there were some things he needed to research first. One of the things was that they were now allowing non-citizens purchase property. The purchaser would buy the property, have it put into and deeded to their name. The purchaser would then be the owner of the property and could build on that property. The purchaser would then be responsible for taking care of that property that was in their name. The problem my friend had to do the research for was. He said that the property was always really owned by the government of that country, but the country was allowing citizens and non-citizens to own that property.

His thoughts were confusing to me. Was my friend really this ignorant of property possession, the rules and regulations of owning property? Did he not understand how to buy and sell property? Maybe he needed a lesson? Maybe he needed to understand how it is and had always been in the United States and I am sure all over the world.

Anyway…………………………..

In the United States of America the government owns the rights to all property within their boundary. Are you getting this? The US government owns all the physical dirt and water within the USA. The US government issues deeds to property. Your grandma, grandpa, mom, and or dad may hold a title or deed to a piece of property. That deed is in their name and valid. They may "own" that property.

What exactly does "own" mean? Own means that the deed or title is in the holders name and documented. By owning the holder is responsible for the upkeep and taking care of that property. In most states within the USA the owner of that property pays taxes on that property every year. That means the holder pays taxes to own that piece of property each year and the holder takes care of that piece of property each year.

How about an example: There is a term called Eminent Domain. You might want to look that up. Eminent Domain means the government has to power to take your deeded or titled property from you or re-use a portion of that titled or deeded property any time it sees fit. For instance, if the state, county, or city wants to put a road through the middle of your property for some reason, they can go through a process and take your property, buy it, or whatever they deem necessary. It happens and you may not really hear about it. It is the same with zoning and re-zoning of existing property. Cities, counties and states do it all the time. They hold meetings where they invite the public to come and share their thoughts, but in the end these boards of administrators already have made plans to carry out whatever they propose they just play the game by inviting the public to share their thoughts. Then the board passes and approves what they were going to in the first place, before you even came to say what you wanted to say.

How about another example: We are all human beings and we think nothing bad will ever happen to us. Right? Until it does. What if you own a piece of property and a section of it, you decide you are not going to mow it for some reason? Depending upon the location of that property you may receive a notice from the city or county telling you to mow it. Telling you that you are responsible for the upkeep. If you say, well it is my property, I will do what I want with it, and I am not going to mow it. You may come home one day and someone mowing it. Do not worry; you will get a bill in the mail for that service. They warned you and you did not heed their advice.

How about another example: Since we think, nothing will ever happen to us. What if you have some property in your name and you forget or do not pay taxes on it one year. You will get some notices surely in the mail. If you do not pay those taxes, your property will come up for sale on the courthouse steps. Whoever pays the taxes on it will have it put into their name and you will need to find another place to live.

How about another example: You own a house, which is on a piece of property. You suddenly go into the hospital. You die that night. You do not have a will expressing whom your property goes to. You are dead. In some instances, the government may seek out your living relatives. Do they have to seek them out? I do not think so. The government does not want your property anyway! All they want is for someone to pay taxes on it every year and keep it up. If there is no extended family to leave the property to, it reverts to the government, city and or state.

In fact, you pay taxes every year to have a title or deed for property to be in your name. You can legally hand it down from generation to generation if that is your desire. However, if it is forgotten or left unmaintained it will most likely revert back to the city and state government for resale.

Therefore, when you drive around to a neighborhood or through a city and you see a piece of property that looks condemned or out of care. If it is still not in the name of the city or county to be sold or torn down. Someone or some entity owns that title or deed and is paying the taxes on it.

It is kind of like rent-to-own and you must follow the rules or it goes back to the government. All they want is for you to pay the taxes and take care of that property until them, the government, finds a use for it and they need it more than you do.

Here is YOUR activity................

Were you aware of this term called eminent domain? It does not matter if you agree with it or not this is how it is in the USA and I would guess all the other countries. Everything goes back to where it started, the government. The government has the final say when it comes to many things and one of those being the property within its borders.

Now that we all area aware of this, how do we propose to keep whatever we (our family) have titles to, to in fact keep those titles within our hands? Can you put together a simple plan of action? Think about 5 things you or a member of your family has in their name. How do you know this? They more than likely get a tax notification in the mail each year.

Mobile: cars, boats, motorcycles, scooters, vans, trucks, camper, trailer, etc.

Static: house, cabin, modular, timeshare, etc.

Did I miss anything? We pay taxes on a lot of items. We pay sales tax when we buy them and sometimes we pay every year to keep them. Some states you pay sales tax when you buy the item once, then you pay a small set fee every year to keep it and or tag it. Some states you pay every year. Insurance is another thing associated with this. Liability and or full coverage. Depending usually upon whether the item is payed off ad owned or has a mortgage.

What is the item 1, 2, 3, 4, and 5?

Is the item paid off?

Liability or full coverage?

Taxes every year or a set fee only every year or both?

## Electronic Fraud

Since this is an election year let's discuss voting. I'm not going to get into politics that isn't my line. This topic can cover any political party: Democrat, Republican, Independent, etc. Even a barrel of monkeys, which I sometimes elude to the political population. The political population that seems to be ran and populated by a bunch of children or monkeys at the zoo. You know, the monkeys at the zoo in cages throwing feces at each other and laughing. That is my idea of a political party.

Anyway, these last several elections have been swamped by conspiracies of supposed voting fraud. One thing I can say is that a conspiracy is only a conspiracy if it has not actually happened or taken place. The second thing I can say is that security is and has never been 100% that does not exist. We talk about that in security classes all the time.

I will ask you this: Do you think that a company that makes millions/billions of dollars each year will have any representative of theirs come on national television and say, "We are as secure as we think we can be but we all know there is no such thing as 100% security".

I have never seen it and I seriously doubt I ever will. That would be an honest evaluation but you and I will never see it! We will never see it as it would be the start of the downfall for that company. That would be a level of honesty that will never happen in a million years.

If this were your company, would you get on national television and announce the flaws? I doubt it. You are a human just like the ones that own and work at these companies. They are not going to bite off the hand that feeds them.

Here is YOUR activity................

What do you think about the topic at hand? What might be a PRO of telling the world how safe YOU think you or your company is and give one CON. In the old days it seemed you could scare off potential threats. Is this prevalent in these current days? Do human elements scare easily or does technology give them some sort of advantage at least in their head? What is your opinion? Would you rather spend a lot of time, energy, and money trying to scare someone off or would you rather spend that time, energy, and money making an example out of them after the fact? Are warnings enough?

## Profiling II

Back when I was younger you could get on a bus, airplane, etc. with a gun. I remember every semester I would take a train from Savannah Georgia to Fort Meyers Florida to stay with my grandparents over the summer. I would always take along one of my shotguns. I would have it on a soft case and take it on the train with my other bag. It has been many years since something like that was permissible to happen.

On another note: I remember when I was in the $8^{th}$ grade in North Little Rock Arkansas in Junior High School we had a show-and-tell one day. Each student brought something from their home related to their family history to class and explained to the other students and their teacher. My great grandfather was in the Civil War on the side of the Union. He was involved in what was later called "The Great Train Robbery". He and several other men in his company and several spies store a Confederate train called the "General". They drove the train from the south and headed up north destroying southern things along the way. Anyway, my grandfather was the $6^{th}$ man to receive the Congressional Medal of Honor (CMH). Matter of fact, the first batch of CMH medals were given to these men along with my grandfather. The sword that my grandfather was presented as a part of the CMH award was the family relic I took to the show-and-tell. I got into trouble for bringing a weapon on that school campus.

One of these stories goes one way and the other story goes the other way. This is why I mention them. My guess, as of today, I doubt very seriously you would get away with taking any form of a weapon on a train, bus, etc. or be able to take any sort of similar item to a show-and-tell on a physical school campus.

These stories bring me to the topic of this writing "profiling".

My taking the train story I was 18 or 19 years old. The show-and-tell story I was 13 years old.

Question: In the first story, I was around 18 years of age. At that time or even currently what 18-year-old white kid has carried out a mass shooting on a train using a shotgun?

Question: In the second story, I was around 13 years of age. At that time or even currently what 13-year-old white kid has carried out a mass stabbing in a school classroom with a sword?

You could call this a type of profiling.

Maybe a little more explanation. Let us reverse the reality!

In the first story: Let us say I was an 18-year-old white kid and I murdered everyone on the train with the shotgun I had brought with me.

So, would you think it be normal to look and review every 18 year old white kid carrying a shotgun on your train before boarding? As he might be a potential threat.

In the second story: Let us say I was a 13 year old white kid and I murdered everyone in my classroom with the sword I brought to class for show-and-tell.

So, would you think it be normal to look and review every 13 year old white kid carrying a sword to class? As he might be a potential threat.

It seems a bit far-fetched, but think about it.

By profiling the past and seeing that, it was an 18 and a 13-year-old white kid that perpetrated these murders. These two would be subject to more scrutiny when trying to board trains and enter classrooms because the past history PROVES this point. This is proof! This is profiling.

Another profiling example:

You may not realize this. Have you ever heard of 9-11? When the airplanes flew into the twin towers in New York City and killed many people. Look it up.

Well, 9-11 caused a LOT of profiling at airports. I mean a lot of profiling that never existed before. Who were the people who got onto these airplanes at the airports? What was their nationality? What did they look like? How were they dressed? They were all men and no women. None of them was White and none of them was Black. They were all lighter-skinned but darker than white. They were all of the same nationality. Right after 9-11 happened if you went to airports you would see the people that fit the physical descriptions of all those who participated in the 9-11 tragedy were detained at airports MORE than anyone else. They were taken aside and put through a more rigorous boarding process than any other persons.

Question: If you were getting ready to be on an airplane would you feel safer knowing that some of those passengers were detained and made 100% sure they would not harm you or take over the plane once it took off and maybe kill you and everyone else on board, or do you not really care and are willing to take the chance that those people are safe? But, we all know there is no such thing as 100% safety and security, but would this profiling make it more safer than the 50%? Does that make sense?

We all want to be safe? Right? As safe as we want to feel we are anyway?

Now, I can see both sides of a profiling issue. You will always have exceptions to every rule. Every person at that airport being screened twice does not have to be a terrorist. Every person at that airport dressed the same way as those 9-11 terrorists does not have to be a terrorist. Every person at that airport that is the same nationality does not nor will all of them be terrorists.

Would you rather be safe than sorry because you did not double-check some of those people who fit the same profile as the 9-11 terrorists that killed all those people?

This is a HUGE topic that covers a lot of ground.

In my opinion. If we can save one single life through profiling and being more cautious then it is worth the inconvenience of anyone within a society. We all have to help as it is the responsibility of all of us as a whole.

Now, that said there is another side effect of profiling.

Does or can it bring about detainment and false imprisonment and incarceration for someone just because of their race or creed. You bet it can. It happens all the time and probably every day. I cannot say this enough, there are good cops and there are bad cops. You cannot have a 100% secure and credible law enforcement force. That does not exist. Anything that is 100% does not exist. You will always have that, I am afraid. You will always have an element of conjecture. I do not care where you are. Nothing is ever 100%.

How about one last scenario. When I was around 22 years old there was a rash of destructions at the local town cemetery. Someone had been going into the cemetery at night breaking headstones, moving markers and stones around. The cemetery gates closed and locked at 8 pm at night but you could walk to just about everywhere around the cemetery and gain entrance, as there was no real fence around it. The cemetery was in the middle of town and many neighborhoods backed up to the cemetery grounds. It was concluded that kids were probably going in there and damaging those things.

The local law enforcement decided that the probable profile of the ones doing the damage were kids or teenagers on foot who may even live in one of the neighborhoods adjacent to the cemetery. For the next week law enforcement took the names down of every kid or teenager they saw walking around the area between the hours of 8 pm at night and until the cemetery opened each morning. By following, this profiling the damage within the cemetery stopped after the first week. This was a positive profiling.

Here is YOUR activity................

We all are aware of profiling scenarios that put profiling in a BAD LIGHT! We hear and or see them every time media wants to bring it to our attention. That seems to be the determining factor. Whether or not the bias party wants to bring it out into the street and make it known or not.

We all want to do good things. Each of us want to be known for doing good things. None of us want to be known for doing anything bad! Who would? Nobody I know. Probably nobody you know either?

Pick a PRO and a CON. Pick a story where profiling was a positive and it saved lives. Pick a story where profiling was a negative and took at least one life.

### Plagiarism

Plagiarism is taking the work of someone else and saying this it is your own work. This is cheating and in a college or university scenario, you typically could be suspended or expelled depending upon the severity of the infraction and the pushing of penalties by the faculty delineating the infraction.

If someone in a class gives their completed assignment and you turn it in as yours, they may also be applicable to the same punishment. A partner in crime so-to-speak. Reading a posting by another student and following his or her post as a guide is also cheating. Using artificial intelligence (AI) to complete and assignments for you is cheating.

Look at it a different way: What if you are a book writer and your family depends upon you to provide for them and someone steals your work instead of paying for it? What if that little amount of money can provide life for one of your children and someone steals it causing your child to die? What do you say then? Yes, it seems a little drastic of a scenario, but you must think of these things, as you never know what could be effected/affected when you do something you know is wrong. Stealing is stealing. Cheating is stealing.

Here is YOUR activity……………..

I WILL SAY IT ONCE AND I WILL SAY IT AGAIN AND AGAIN. "Don't start something and you won't have to worry about it catching up to you in the end".

Don't start stealing and it will never be on your mind to look back over your shoulder. Don't start plagiarizing as you will end up doing the same thing, being paranoid that someone is always watching you and that you will never know when they surface.

What have I said before: "There are two people on this planet. When bad things happen to them. One that says, why me, what have I done to deserve this? And the other that says, it was a matter of time, I was expecting it". Who do you want to be?

DO NOT START IT AND YOU WILL NOTY EVEN NED TO WASTE TIME THINKING ABOUT IT!

We all get tired and lazy at some point. This is the nature of the human element. Just one very easy and simple slip can cost us a great deal if someone wants to pursue and make an example of us plagiarizing and or cheating. It is very easy to do. IS it worth the risk a moment of weakness? A moment of justifying and minimizing what we are about to do.

It does not matter if you agree with the penalties of cheating and or plagiarism they are there for a purpose. The purpose is to hinder or stop plagiarism! It is to scare the participant into thinking twice. I assure you there have been a myriad of careers ruined by a mistake, a mistake you are warned about repeatedly.

If you have cheated in the past and got away with it, this is for you. If not, you have no idea. That is good, as you don't have to watch your back every minute of every day.

I'm not looking for confessions. I'm just making sure everyone is aware of the consequences of their actions. To take responsibility.

DO you have a story to tell? Maybe you tried and got caught? Did you learn anything? Can you relate to what I am trying to say?

## Disaster Recovery Plan (DRP)

What is a DRP? It is a plan put together for instances which may occur through a disaster. Some of these can be man-made deliberate, man-made accidental, and or Acts of God or Mother Nature if you like to hold her accountable instead.

What happens when a disaster strikes? Who is in charge? Do specific roles change of individuals with the existing company structure? Who decides whether it is a cold, warm, or hot site? Does everyone run around like a chick with their head cut off or is there a delineated plan of attack? Would it be nice if your company had a strategy or plan if a disaster did strike? Most people like structure.

Any company big or small. It does not necessarily have to be a company at all. It can be you or your own personal family. Do you have a plan in place if a disaster were to happen within your family? Would part of a family disaster plan be that everyone have a "living will"? A living will that explains exactly what should happen to you and or your body if something happens to you to where you cannot speak or transcribe your wishes. Many families currently still think, "It will not happen to me, until it does". Then sometimes it is too late.

Here is YOUR activity……………..

Come up with a simple scenario where you might need a DRP? Maybe something in your personal life that could have went better if there was a plan put into place before the disaster came about? It can be simple and or complex as you need it to be. Can the death of a loved one near us be a disaster? Do you realize how much a single death within our inner-circle cause's problems or issues to arise? Things you never really realized were associated. You really didn't understand how many PIES that person had their hands into.

How many lives were associated with that person? Titles, bank accounts, charge accounts, etc. If you sat down with a piece of paper and listed ONLY things YOU were involved with how long would that list be? I was talking with my sister the other day about me writing up a list for myself. If I were to die all my assets would be tied up and no one could get to them unless they were given access. I really need to do that! As do us all! I have talked about for years me getting a living will or a will. I have yet to take time to do it. As I am a human entity, and I think it will never happen to me! But, alas, one day it will as it will happen to all of us.

## Infrastructure

Do you realize how many networks are available that we use every day? There are gas, electric, water, telephone, garbage, etc. for utilities. There are television, cable, intranet, internet, satellite, etc. There are physical city, county, state, interstate and intrastate roadways. There are bridges and tunnels. There are physical wired networks and wireless networks. There are physical copper telephone networks and cellular telephone networks. There are airline, bus, taxi, train, travel interstate, intrastate, and international travel and transit networks. These are just a few off the top of my head.

How often are any of these updated or remodeled? Do you even have any idea? Do you hear of any of them in the news or in commercials?

Let us take for instance the cellular telephone network. Does your cell phone ever act weird? Have you ever been in the middle of a call and the call was dropped/stopped? Do your ever hear noises or clipping in the background of your conversation? Has anyone ever complained to you that your voice is not as clear as it usually is or that your voice is chirping? Why do you think this is happening? Do you have a newer model cell phone? Do you have a want or a need to buy a newer model phone as you think it will solve your connection issues?

Think about this:

For one thing, the cellular telephone infrastructure has not been thoughtfully maintained since it was first implemented. It has had limited updating and version changes since it was implemented.

Just within the United States how many cell phones do most of the people around you have just within your small inner circle? Your inner circle of friends. Do some of those friends have two or more cell phones each? One for personal, and maybe one for work and maybe another for some other reason? Maybe an iPad or tablet or a laptop. What it boils down to is how many of these devices connect to a network? They may all or most of them share the same network connection. You do realize they all connect and share the same data stream. When multiple devices share the same stream they can cause and will cause bottlenecks. A bottleneck is when a lot of somethings try to share the same path. If that is a 1 Gb stream then all the devices share a portion or piece of that stream. If 10 devices share the stream then that 1 Gb is split into 10, each getting 1/10$^{th}$ of that stream.

Every time a company wants us to purchase something new they give it a different number. Remember when the data was proposed to be 1 Gb in speed. Remember when the data supposedly was upgraded to 1 2Gb speed. Remember when they wanted us to buy the 3 Gb package and now we hear of the 5 Gb plans. Remember all of these?

It is a researchable fact that these have all been ploys to get money from the public. Of course, the shareholders in these companies are extremely happy as times have been good for them, but as far as the public, they have suffered from the lies espoused from the sales representatives and marketers.

Test the speed of any device on a network. Review your upload and download speeds. Are these in the range of speed you were told you are paying for that monthly fee that always seems to have some surcharge added to it? It is highly doubtful.

Example: I have had issues for months and really even years but these seem to grow more and more as time goes on. I have had others tell me of my phone connections and they tell me I really need to upgrade my phone. So, I call my cell provider and ask what would be a good model to upgrade to. I explained what I use my phone for and I want something similar. The phone support person asks why I want to upgrade. I tell her what all my friends say and they think I need a new phone. She says I currently have this model and my best and closest upgrade would be the cell phone model I already have as it is one of their most popular models. She says she sees no need for me to upgrade the cell phone I currently have as it would just be me spending money for the same phone I have. I thank her for her advice and stall have that same phone today.

I put on my thinking cap with what she told me. The problem isn't with my cell phone the problem is with the service. The service has not been upgraded for the amount of users sharing the data streams. That is the issue and problem. There isn't enough towers and streams available for all that sharing.

Think about this too: How about another example:

How about the road networks you travel each day. Have you ever blown out a tire or bent a rim on a car or had to have your vehicle front end re-aligned from a pothole you drove into? You do realize that if you pay taxes part of what you is supposed to pay to have those potholes fixed. How many years are they there until they finally fix that hole? Tax dollars at work.

Are there any networks that you see are deteriorating around you? Give two examples that you physically see with details and how those networks involve you as a tax-paying citizen. Are you getting what you pay for?

## P l a n n i n g

Do you realize you can plan, sometimes you can plan a lot, sometimes you can plan too little and sometimes you just can't plan out anything at all? Sometimes it might not be under your control.

Example: I had surgery yesterday at 2:00 pm. I got there an hour early and went through the procedures as expected. Well, I didn't really know what to expect 100% but I had an idea. Maybe you are too young to realize that sometimes the anesthetic you take during a surgery can take your life. It does sometimes happen in real life. That is one of those curious things that you hope for a decent outcome.

Everything went okay and we left for home. Both of my sisters were with me as I had to have one with me at all times during the surgery and after as I had pain medicines and I could not drive. Four pain pills a day for up to 30 days if needed. Anyway, on the way home we decided to stop and get something to eat as I had not eaten since the night before at about 8 pm. We stopped and ate. After eating I had a strange feeling in my throat. My throat was swollen and felt harder than normal. I didn't have any idea why, as during the anesthesia process the first of my surgery there was only an air tube in my nose and nothing in my throat. That would be normal I guess as I am sure they would not want to scare you by putting that long tube down your throat while you were awake. It was probably put in after that point, but nobody ever said anything. It was just a given I guess.

I had my sisters feel the swelling and they noticed it wasn't normal and we left for home. They didn't just take me home and drop me off they came in for a while. The discharge paperwork said I needed someone with me for the next 24 hours at least. Anyway, they both have responsibilities at their own houses so I don't know about myself being babysat for 24 hours. That was questionable.

We sat around a talked a while. They decided they would go home and change clothes and let their dogs out and bring back something for supper. They said they would bring back whatever I wanted that they were not hungry. They came back an hour later and had brought back supper and they decided they would just share something and hang around for a while before they went home. The plan was for them to drop it off and go home.

I opened the lid and took a few bites. My throat was still swollen. I drank some water and had a hard time getting it to go down my throat. I drank more water and it went down. I took a few more bites and the same thing happened again. I always chew really well but something was happening. I drank and took a few breaths. I took a couple of small bites and all of a sudden I could not breathe. It was like my throat had closed up after those last bites. I sat there for a second thinking of what I needed to do. "I was a scuba diver when I was younger and I can hold my breath a really long amount of time and I am really good with patience under the water as I learned how to extremely remain calm and slow my breathing to a very low minimum. This really worked out by being able to do this". I got up and stood by my kitchen sink. I could feel a little air coming through. I tried to drink some water but it was painful and would not push anything down my throat. I stood there thinking, what to do next. They are asking if I want to call 911. I can't say anything I just say no with my hands and arms. I'm still gasping for air. I try to talk and cam only really speak with my motions from my hands.

It is pretty rough by now, and I motion and try to say I am choking and I need someone to out their arms around my chest from behind and pull. One of my sisters gets behind me, locks her hand together and pulls and does the Heimlich maneuver. The food goes down and I can breathe again. If they had dropped supper off and left me alone I would not be writing this. When my sister came over this morning to check on me at 3:30 am she would have found me dead. You just never know and sometimes you can never plan enough.

Right after all has turned out well, my sister said "If that pull would not have worked the next pull would have pulled me off of the ground!" FUNNY, how the human element can always find a joke out of a possible tragedy. Well, that was my learning experience #974 and close call to death about #15. haha...

Here is YOUR activity................

Have you ever heard of or been involved in a similar story? Does this make sense? There are no human elements on this earth currently that are perfect. There is no one that knows everything. Bad things can happen to good people and good things can happen to bad people. I guess it is just the luck of the draw. The luck of the draw in that hand of cards each of us are dealt. What do you think? Maybe something you know of happened to have a good result because of something done or not done?

## S y m b i o t i c

I'm not going to copy and paste a definition for symbiotic, anyone can do that. I will explain it as how I see it. When I think of symbiotic I see an acquired relationship that is mutually pleasing. If you have two human entities who propose to be in a symbiotic relationship then I would assume the inputs of both parties combine into a positive output. Two human entities working together for the common goal of success.

And we can relate this term to security as well. Symbiotic relationships could be construed as a best practice. Good things are best practices.

If we are truly born knowing nothing and we become products of our environments through the relationships we encounter in our lives along the way, then it only goes to say that the symbiotic relationships we become entangled in are the ones who aid us in being all-we-can-be and in-fact prosperous. Symbiotic is reciprocal, kind of like, the wheel gets grease when it starts to squeak. If you need help "Symbiotic" comes to your aid.

Maybe some of us are old enough to remember words of supposed wisdom. Wisdom that someone in our past presents to us through a past discussion or discussions. One of those being, "does that relationship drag you to the bottom or allow you to float"?

There are many relationships we enter into through the duration of our lives, some of those are by our own choice and some of those are by the choice of others we allow. We give them that control. We pass that "our control" onto them. Sometimes, we feel like we have no choice. Is the choice ours to give in the first place? Put on your thinking hat.

The symbiotic positive relationships are the ones we as humans strive for. These are the ones that make us stand tall and put us on a pedestal for others to see. "Look at me, here I am" With your help I made it". I made it through the shark and barracuda infested waters, with your assistance, I made it.

We all have things in life that bring us down and make us sad. These things keep us grounded. These are the things that keep us on the narrow path to success. There are pitfalls along the way we must step over and bypass. These thinks keep us aware of how things can possibly go if we do not strive to keep them down and keep them chained until we want to deal with them.

No matter how bad something might be, it can always be worse. Right? Whenever I get to feeling bad or how bad something I see Is, I think of how things could be. I think of how bad something could be.

Example: One of my best friends had had cancer several times. She is my age. It seems that every few years she has to have the cancer removed then it always comes back for another round, and here she goes having it removed again. Several times now. I just think of how it must be for her to go through Chemotherapy every several years and having body parts amputated. My problems seem small in comparison.

Example: My mother has beaten cancer six times. Six times in different parts of her body. My problems seem small in comparison

Example: My mother again. My mother was born with small blood pathways to her eyes. Ten years ago these flared up and she lost sight in one of her eyes. She was made legally blind at that time. This was difficult, for us all as we grew up reading, reading, and reading as a family. This ended abruptly. Anyway, she had 60% sight in the remaining eye. This is the tenth year. Every month, like clockwork, she has a needle injection into the center of that eye to keep the inflammation down. If she skips an eye injection by even one single day she risks losing the rest of the eye permanently. My problem are small in comparison.

I have many, many other examples. I think you get the point. No matter how bad somethings are or at least seem to be, sometimes they are not as bad as we portray them or they could always be worse.

Here is YOUR activity................

Do you have any ideas or thoughts on this matter? Have you ever thought the end of the world was coming only to find it wasn't that bad to begin with? Our minds can sometimes play unbelievable tricks upon us. All is sometimes not lost! Sometimes, we just need to sit back and think for a time. Develop a plan or a strategy to override this disaster we think has befallen us.

## R e s p e c t

Pay attention. This topic has several tangents so bare/bear with me so you learn something from this activity.

When I owned my company I had crews that spent years in New Jersey, New York, and Pennsylvania. Some were in the cities and some were on the islands. I had several crews that had just returned the week before the 9-11 disaster in downtown New York. I was watching the events unfold on the television during the disaster, minute by minute.

Previous to 9-11 most of the time my crews found certain restaurants they liked and continued going to those during their stay in those areas. Quite a few of the restaurant staff and owners grew accustomed to my people gathering at those facilities. Quite a few of my employees were the sons and daughters of veterans on Korea and Vietnam, as well as myself. The majority of us over the years had gotten hand-me-downs from our fathers, uncles, and grandpas who were veterans of foreign wars. These hand-me-down tokens were usually in the form of jackets or ball caps, generally green in color or derivatives of camouflage with military branch insignia attached. These were forms of each of our family histories.

This was strange: Early in our time spent in the northern cities we would enter a restaurant and the staff would take our whole crew to the back of the restaurant away from all the other customers. We found this really strange. Why were we being swept away back into the corner? What was the problem?

After a few months my people spoke up and asked why we were treated the way they were. The staff said that it was because the clothing they wore. Like I mentioned earlier in this writing military green coats and hats were the choice of dress for my teams. The staff continued to say that the area we were in was a high area for gang activity and several of the gangs in that area wore military clothing and colors. By sitting my company team members in the back of the restaurant was to keep an issue from happening if a rival gang member was to walk by the windows of the diner and see them sitting there wearing their gang colors. She continued to say that drive by shooters were a common happening in that area and they were trying to keep something like that from happening. Now, it all makes sense. She was stopping a potential issue from happening by placing my people away from the front windows of the establishment.

There was nothing against my people, the staff just wanted to stay away from trouble.

Quite often I see a teenager walking down a sidewalk and paying attention only to the screen on their cell phone. Sometimes they walk into the person walking towards them. They seem to have not a care in the world and little to no respect for anyone else.

I was sitting at a café in downtown New York one day. It was a nice day and I was sitting out at the sidewalk at a table. I always look around and pay attention to my surroundings. I watch the people coming and going. I was watching this teenager this particular day. He was all entranced on the screen of his cell phone. Not paying attention to anyone or anything around him. Heading towards him directly in front of him was a gang member. I don't remember if he wore blue of red colors. He was either a Crip or a Blood, I don't remember.

The teenager walked directly into the gang member. The gang member grabbed his phone and threw it into the street into the oncoming traffic. It went under a taxi and was ran over and destroyed. The gang member never took his eyes off the teenager. He was waiting for him to say something, anything. The teenager just stood there. The gang member walked off. It was hard to control my laughter. The gang member was walking toward my table. He just looked straight ahead and walked on by.

I guess this was learning experience #54 for the teenager. I hope he learned from that experience. All, I can say at this time is that if the shoe was on the foot of another teenager, you would not say anything either. I don't think a cell phone is worth the possible infliction of pain. Have some respect for the people around you. You are breathing their air too. Watch where you are walking.

Here is YOUR activity................

Have you ever heard of an incident as this? Do you pay attention to your surroundings? Do you care what others think around you? Do you think the world revolves solely around you? Have you ever heard of audience participation? Isn't that really what life is anyway? Life is just one big audience trying to participate with each other, sometimes positively and sometimes negatively? Can't we all just get along? What do you think? Do we all earn respect or are we just born with this intimate object called respect. Is it given to us or do we earn it? At what point in our lives does it all combine and we receive it?

# Research

I could have called this many things and I chose research as the title. Research is one of those things in life we all have to do ourselves. We cannot take it for granted that what another human entity says to us is the honest truth. If you do, you will have a long row-to-hoe in your life that probably would not have been as difficult if you did a little research.

Since the day we are born we gather knowledge we see, hear, and feel from our surroundings. Whether we like it or not we build bias along the way. Some may be positive and some may be negative, but all together we build a base of bias. Every single human entity on this planet attains and retains this. The older we get the more we build. Maybe some of our bias change along the path through our own research and or our gathering of knowledge from our relationships and surroundings.

Do your own research. Just because you take a class on X does not mean the instructor or professor is the single entity you are supposed to learn that topic from. If you really want to learn, then learn. Learning is your job as a student. It is your job as a student to do more than the minimum and to research and learn additions from whatever sources you search out.

Example: We all say we want to vote for the right candidate as President of the United States. Do you just listen to what others have to say about a candidate or do you really take the time to research that candidate and find out for ourselves if they are the right candidate for us. What the ones around us say may not be correct at all. In this day and age news is all around us, fake and real, made-up and honest. Think about it. Everybody and their brother has an opinion. Everyone has a bias, newspaper editors, reporters, talk show hosts, newscasters, etc. They all have a bias and who they work for will also have bias too. Who signs their paycheck? Think about it. Do your research before you have an opinion it could save you a lot of re-canting in the end.

Don't take the word from someone else as true, your life just might depend upon it. Are you willing to trust your life on the word of someone else?

In all honesty I would have died several times by now if I had listened to what someone else said.

One example: When I was younger a lot of my friends had big tall four wheel drive trucks. We would all hang out together pretty much anywhere there was a mud hole. I had 44 inch tall mud tires called Ground Hawgs. These were almost four feet high. I had to climb up on the tire to get into the cab of the truck. You could stand in the bed of the truck and reach up and smack the stoplight at an intersection. It was really high and powerful.

Anyway, on weekends we would all gather together and meet at a place called the pipeline. The pipeline was where acres and acres of land was excavated and gas pipelines were ran for miles. This was a mud fiasco. Miles and miles of mud pits and hills and valleys. There would be a hundred vehicles running the trails, dirt bikes, dune buggies, rock crawlers, mud trucks, three and four wheelers, everyone out getting muddy from dawn to dark.

One of my first times there I had two friends riding in my truck with me. One of them said he had been up there many times. I kind of trusted what he said but did I really? All through my life I have always kind of had a sick-sense you might say, maybe a little man on my shoulder. A little man on my shoulder that would pop up when I might be getting ready to do something really-really stupid. I have been saved quite a few times by this invisible entity.

We are in my truck going up and down these hills, mountains really. They were all about a 45 degree incline, then you would come down the other side at a 45 degree angle. Up and down, up and down, up and down. It was getting rather late and the sun was getting ready to go down and we were traveling along. We seemed to be going straight up this one last mountain and the sun was gone and all I could see ahead of us was the sky. I said I could not see anything, all I could see is sky. My friend said don't worry I have been up here a hundred times and we are fine, keep going, keep going, we are fine.

The little man on my shoulder said to stop. I stopped just at the crest of the hill. There was nothing in front of us but blue sky. I locked the brake and we got out. We walked ten feet ahead and looked over a cliff that was 300 feet high. There was no other side to that hill, it was straight down. There is a moral to this story. I will never forget it. That is just one of my stories, I could write a book of the many others.

Here is YOUR activity................

Did you ever make a bad decision because you listened to someone else and took their advice? Did you ever think about something, make a decision, and then change your mind before doing it and it turned out to be the right decision? How about the wrong decision? If you are young enough to remember: Did someone make a right or wrong decision for you?

## Business Continuity Plan (BCP)

In short a BCP is a plan that is put together to keep everyone on the same page. To try to make sure things go as projected, expected, or planned. To make sure a business flows with as little hick-ups as possible. You will always encounter unexpected hick-ups but it is good to try to at least limit them whenever possible. Preventative maintenance so-to-speak. A little foresight can save a ton of hind-sight.

Some businesses are small and start out with little to nothing and grow along the way. This is fine for a small entity as you learn from experience and as you grow. You learn from your failures and mistakes, the learning experiences. But, if you have a large company with a lot of employees you want to leave very few things to chance, very few things to conjecture or guesswork. What if you had a company and everything was whatever anyone wanted to do at the time? It was all open to whoever thought whatever and whomever did whatever, however they wanted to do it. It would seem to turn out to somewhat of a mess I would guess.

Did you get a loan from a bank to start your venture? How long can you exist and pay employees when everyone does as they please and there is no structure or accountability. Can everyone just blame everyone else? Is anyone making money to put back in the company and pay the payroll? You need a plan. A plan of action. This plan is similar to a disaster recovery plan (DRP). A DRP is a documented plan of attack during a disaster which directly relates to getting the business back up and running. The BCP is the plan that delineates the structure of that business. We could say the BCP is in place as a form of preventative maintenance before the fact and the DRP is after the disaster has occurred getting the company operating back to normal.

Here is YOUR activity................

Imagine you have started a company and you have very limited cash on hand. You are new to the business game. You have found a niche to make money and have decided to jump on it. List five essential things in detail you think need to be in place to start your venture. There are some items YOU must have in place and some things you can learn along the way. List five things in detail you think you can learn along the way after starting your venture.

# Assumptions

This is college, YOUR time going to k-12 classrooms is over. It is time to think like an adult and come to the realizations of an adult. Put YOUR cell phone down and pay attention!

Security……………………..

"YOU never know unless you ask. Speak up and ask! Don't assume anything!"

Have you ever heard anyone say "There is NO such thing as a dumb question"?

Well, it might be……if…….the teacher, instructor, or professor just said something and YOU were not listening or paying attention. THEN, I THINK it becomes a dumb question!

All through life we have what I call "learning experiences". These are the day-to-day things we run into each day of our lives. You know, some of the stupid things we do, sometimes we get away with them unharmed and other we get caught and penalized. I don't care how young or old you are you do these, some of us more than others.

Here comes my point!

Did you ever do something wrong? Did you ever THINK you knew how to do something and you did it, then you found out you did it the wrong way? If you had only asked how to do it the right way you might have come out okay. All because you were too shy or too proud or too whatever to ask. Does that make sense?

If YOU had ONLY asked in the first place...BUT NO......YOU thought YOU knew the answer...BUT apparently, you did not!

The word STUBBORN comes to mind.

Did you ever make a mistake and look stupid or dumb because YOU failed to ask a few questions to begin with? Do you always read the directions? In full? Before attempting to do something like an assignment? Have you ever submitted an assignment only to find you did it wrong and the fault is yours because you did not follow the directions? What if the life of someone was ended because YOU did not follow the directions to the letter? Seems a bit far-fetched, right. BUT, what if? These things happen all the time.

You have a gun in the house. You THINK everyone in the house is old enough to know not to play with it, right. Well, I have news for you.

When I was a senior in high school. I was with one of my friends and we went over to the house of one of his friends for some reason. We walked up the steps, my friend was first through the door in front of me. I was behind him. We walked inside the trailer. Beside the door was a rifle standing and leaning against the wall. My friend reached down and picked up the rifle and pointed at his friend's wife who was sitting in a reclined. This really happened really fast! Really fast!

He pointed at his friend's wife, then pointed the rifle into the air and said "Don't worry they never keep guns loaded in the house!" He pulled the trigger and HE WAS WRONG the bullet ripped through the roof of the trailer! Apparently, they had just come home from hunting earlier that day and didn't have time to unload the guns. SHE would be dead and he would have accidentally killed her! That was in 1982 my senior year of high school.

I will never forget the quiet right after that bullet ripped through the roof of that trailer! The shock and awe and the look on everyone's face! I will never forget it!

THINK……………..

I am not asking if you have ever done of been involved in anything as stupid as this. This could have been tragic!

How about another story:

One of my best friends in high school was a Karate student. Had been going to the dojo for years. He was a typical good looking guy, a sports guy, on the football team and other stuff as well. He was kind of a show off and a hot head sometimes.

Anyway, someone told him that one of the guys on our bus had said something about his girlfriend. That day on the bus we were each being dropped off at our houses. The guy who supposedly said something was a kind of friend of mine too. Anyway, the guy who supposedly said something got off the bus and my other friend followed him. He was supposedly defending the honor of his girlfriend. Really, it was just a power thing from my hot head show-off friend. Before anyone knew it my friend had kicked the guy in the face and the guy was kneeling on the ground blood pouring out of his nose. He asked what the problem was and my friend said he was talking about his girlfriend. The guy said no he wasn't and hadn't said anything.

Anyway….Come to find out later, someone just said that and my other friend got kicked in the face for nothing! He had not said anything! Do you know, my friend NEVER apologized for kicking the guy in the face for doing nothing! There are people like that in the world! More than you realize I would wager.

IT WAS ALL A BIG MISTAKE!

Here is YOUR activity…………….

What is you feedback and you thoughts about this? Do you have any experiences you might share with others in this discussion? Sometimes we make decisions when we do not have all the details.

IN BOTH OF THESE SCENARIOS………….Both participants THOUGHT they knew the correct answer and were WRONG! They ASSUMED and were wrong! That is problem with ASSUMPTIONS! Don't assume you know an answer if you really KNOW you do not!

## Marketing

Where can I start a discussion on marketing? Marketing is the backbone of free enterprise and what you might call capitalism. Letting the public population know you have an item or items for sale. If you do not advertise your product then how does someone/anyone know it has been developed and is for sale? This all revolves around a marketing plan or campaign. It isn't free and it can take quite a bit of work. The more you advertise the more people hear about it. You cannot just spend the time, energy, and money for research, development, and manufacture and just let those items sit in a warehouse and not tell the population how and where to get them.

You cannot take it for granted that the advertising or commercials are 100% accurate or honest. They may be accurate and honest on one side of the issue and the other side it may be lacking. A company is not going to spend myriads of dollars telling you what is wrong with their product. They will just not mention those issues at all in their marketing. They will sway from anything related that might bring those issues to the forefront. This is where the research comes in from the potential purchaser. It is the consumer who needs to be aware. It is the consumer that needs to do their diligent research. Sometimes all is not what it seems. A good marketer can portray a half empty glass as half full and vice-versa. That is their job and what they are paid for.

There will not be a commercial on television or radio that some company is not paying for. Think about the social media platforms we use for free. They really are not free. If they are truly free, why do we get stuck with pop-up ads all the time? These companies pay for pop-up ads. Just think about it. How many items are you made aware of for sale, lease, or rent every single day that you did not expressly sign up for? These companies track you behind the scenes and send you things all the time, and you really do not realize it. This is big business. Selling your name, phone number, e-mail address, home address, birthday, etc. You can run but you cannot hide if you have internet, a cellular telephone, and or even a newer model vehicle. You are being tracked every mile you drive, every step you take, and every conversation or text you make. Welcome to the wide world of advertising and marketing. You are not in control of this.

I have been around for quite a few years now and things we were told years ago that were bad for us and that we should steer away from that caused disease, harm, or maybe even death, over the years they seem to not mention the negatives of those anymore, as they still sell them daily and unaware people buy them. It is all marketing to the unaware. A key here is research, research everything if you need to.

I remember growing up and they said aluminium pans for cooking caused Alzheimer's. The older you get the worse it gets. They still market, advertise and sell these every day. The Teflon coating they said caused us harm. They sell them every day. They said cellular towers caused radiation which caused cancer. Not to build your house next to one, not to send you kids to a school next to one, etc. They do it every day. They just don't talk about it. Don't hold a cell phone up to your ear or next to your brain as those radio transmission waves cause radiation which causes cancer. I see it every day.

Marketing on a new cell phone plan. Within the world we cannot keep up with the infrastructure of the old cell phone plans. We hear about 1G, 2G, 3G, 4G, 5G, when does it stop. Within the world many places still lack 1G.

Do some speed tests? Cell phone and internet, uploads and downloads. In marketing to make money there is no money in customers keeping their same phone, the money is in upgrading. All the flashing light advertisements that get you to buy the new product is expensive. Somebody has to pay for it. The customer pays for it. A good marketing campaign can sell an Eskimo an ice pack. They really can. They do every day. That is never going to stop.

Look at the television commercials right now. Commercials for pills and medicines for diseases, weight loss, etc. If you pay attention, lawyers have commercials on those same stations talking about the after effects of those same medicines and pills, and to hire them for reparations. Really. I see them every day. There is little to no accountability. Some things you cannot advertise in the USA but you can buy it from another country or go across the US border and buy it. Anyway, I am getting off track here.

Here is YOUR activity................

Marketing and advertising is big business. There is a slogan that has been around since I was little "The Buyer Beware". It is the responsibility of the consumer to be safe. Do you ever do research before buying anything? Do you just take the word of someone else or some flashy campaign? Did you ever buy anything that was not really as advertised? Have you ever wasted money on something that you finally found was just a waste? How do you keep from wasting your money? Did you ever want something so bad and you ended up not getting it for some reason, then a little while later it really didn't matter as you didn't care about that item anymore? Do you pay attention to all the hype and flashing light of advertising?

## D e a t h

This is one of those topics that nobody wants to talk about. This is one of those topics that everyone needs to talk about! That is part of the problem I believe. Death comes to the door of every human entity at some point. We don't like him, we do not have to invite him in, and he just shows up and takes us away. I was always told when someone passes away: "It isn't who you will miss when they pass it is who will miss you". That pretty much sums up whether or not you were a good person I guess.

I talk about this topic as it has a relationship to security. If you have one single person that knows how to do a job at a facility, and that person passes, who can fill their shoes? Who know exactly what they did each day? Can you find their replacement the very next day? Is there a plan for that type of disaster? Is there someone cross-trained to do their job if this form of disaster strikes? It will at some point. Death could be considered a disaster in certain situations, not that it isn't in the first place for whomever knew him/her.

Preparation, planning, business continuity plans, disaster recovery plans, many thing in industry are affected/effected by death.

The older we get the more contact we come with death. Our friends, family, pets, are all at the mercy of death. Death can make or break us. Every human entity on this planet of ours has a limit. A limit of what they can mentally and physically take. If you want my honest opinion: If someone close to you passes away don't keep it in. Let it out. Tell people around you. Talk about it. Come to the realizations that you would miss not speaking to others. It is a sad thing and everyone else knows this is a sad event. For the most part I think most people want to help other people. It makes people feel good to be helpful.

If something has put you in a bond people want to know, they need to know, or they cannot help you. Nobody can help you if they do not know what is wrong! Sure, you might cry, oh well, we all cry. Crying is one of those things we need to do when we need to do it. It gives us a sense of cleansing. Saving up your tears does not help anything!

I have so many examples. Too many to list. Every year that goes by I have at least two deaths to personally deal with. I don't like. I wonder when I will have enough. When will I see enough? That is the part of life I do not like. But that is the side of life that is always present.

Example: One of my uncles was drafted into Vietnam. He did his tours and came back home. He saw so much death. He came back home and stayed in the bedroom of his mom and dad's house and pretty much never came out. They would leave food trays outside his door and pick them up when he was done. His mom and dad have both passed away and nobody in the family really knows anything about him. We are just told to leave him alone and that he does not want to be bothered. You might not believe how many thousands of others that came home and did the same as him and some are still alive today.

Example: For many years I have rescued dogs. For some reason I like hound dogs. Right now at the writing of this I have a Beagle and a Walker Treeing Coon Hound, Josie and Belle. I know one day I will have to let them pass along too. I won't like it. I don't even really like to talk or think about it but I know I have to and that is the only absolute of life. That one day they will pass or they may get in a shape and I will have to put them down. That is something I had to do last year to one of my other dogs Marlee. That is the hardest thing I have ever had to do in my life, but I knew I could not let her suffer any longer. It still bothers me now. Who would do the task if not me? It was my responsibility.

I have many more examples, but I think you get the point. If you have had me in classes before I have had announcements about some of these things. We are all the same inside. I think anyway. Some of us are harder and some are softer.

Here is YOUR activity................

I am sure by now if you are at least 20 years of age you are familiar with death. I had a sister who died when she was three days old. The hospital left the widow open and she died of pneumonia. I was in an incubator at the time. I was a premature baby of six months and was in an incubator over a year struggling to survive. I weighed less than five pounds.

Anyway, what are you thinking after reading this? You must have some things?

## B u l l y i n g

Back when I was little I was picked on. I was a small child. I was a premature baby of six months and spent the first year of my life in an incubator at the hospital. Nine months into the incubator I had a sister, she was also premature, she died after three days, the hospital staff left the window open in March and she caught pneumonia.

Some things when I was little I remember. I don't know why some of those things stick in my head and others I don't remember. When I was really little I had a friend that lived in the Cardinal hospital which was a hospital for crippled and disabled children. I would go see him there some days. We lived close by. He could not walk and had braces on both of his legs. I remember telling him that I was crippled too, that when I got home at night my parents would take my legs off and put them in the closet. I never knew why I told him that, but I remember it.

Also, when I got a little older as a teenager and beyond I would always have these dreams, and in these dreams I was always being chased by somebody. The part of the dreams that always stood out was that in my dreams I was crippled and had a hard time running.

There was something wrong with my legs. I never understood why until about ten years ago.

I'm getting older and I stand on my feet a lot and walk a lot. The older I get the more my feet seem to hurt. Now, all night long my legs hurt when I am in bed trying to sleep. About ten years ago I finally realized what my issue was with my feet and why I had those dreams growing up. When I was born one of my feet are flat and the other one has a high arch. When I was really small I wore special shoes to compensate for my arches. They were called "patent leather" shoes. Because they were black, very shiny, and very hard. They had special insoles to adapt for the arches in my feet.

During elementary school we lived in the projects, what you might call government housing. I was picked on at the playground whenever I was at the swing set. I remember one time a guy called "big david" slammed a swing into my mouth and busted it really good. That was just one instance. He was the project bully.

What does this have to do with bullying? Well, I think it has a lot to do with my situation as I was a small child and often got made fun of by the other children. In my early life this made me a certain way. I was small and very shy. I didn't like being made fun of. During elementary school, and junior high school I would never participate in the physical education or gym classes. I would never dress-out and participate. I always got low grades in those grades and sports.

I never ate lunch at school with all the other kids. I would just sit in the classrooms until lunch was over. It wasn't until I got into high school that things began to change. I guess all children have the growth spurts where your body starts to change and you get bigger. Well I got bigger.

During high school this guy sat behind me and was always pocking the back of my neck with a pencil. Every day he just had to give me the routine. I don't remember his name. The teacher I guess would never see anything and I would never tell anyway as I didn't want to be a tattle tale or cause more trouble. One day I had enough. I got up from my desk, and had my book in my hand. It was a big and thick hard book. I disrupted the class. I raised the book and told him if he ever stuck that pencil up to my neck again I would "brain" him with that book. I don't think he ever touched me again. I was bigger than him anyway. He was just picking and could get away with it, until I put a stop to it, I guess.

Enough examples. Bullying isn't just something like I have been speaking of like intimidation it can also be in a form as blackmail, extortion, coercion or threats. Threatening someone to do something "or else". "Or else" I will tell on you for something I saw you do, or I will make up a story that you did something you did not do, or just about anything else.

I think back then was quite a bit different than now. If you look back in history. Times just become different. Maybe every 30, 40, or 50 years things just seem to get different for some reason. I think the reason is technology. The more technologically advanced we get the easier life becomes for us, the human entities. I think bullies, or the different types of bullies change with those times. Technology makes different bullies. Those technologies provide more access to human entities through those technologies.

Maybe the human elements have always been somewhat the same but the technologies make the availability more prevalent and accessible.

Think about bullies and technology advancement.

I do think however, bullies come from somewhere. A bully just isn't born. A bully is nurtured and developed from their surroundings and previous relationships. Something made the bully into a bully. Parents, friends, home life, it could be pretty much anything.

In my opinion something makes a bully a bully. Is the father or mother of the bully their bully? Is their sister or brother their bully? Is their friend their bully? Who bullies them? I do not think it is just a one-stop deal being a bully. No matter how big you are there is always someone, somewhere bigger than you! No matter how tough you are there is always someone, somewhere tougher than you!

If you are the bully you are not the only person holding the "bully" torch. There are many others just like you. All through my life and even now my friends and I that I grew up with, we talk about the bullies of our past. We sit around and laugh about it. The funny part is that usually we knew a bully and knew someone else that came along and took care of the bully. "What comes around goes around". There is always some bigger. We always seem to think that those bullies were a part of our lives that helped to make us who we are today.

Maybe if we didn't physically see the faults of those bullies then we might not have turned into the people we are today? Maybe we could have been bullies if we had no bullies that kept us down? If we are honest, caring human entities when we get older is that because of the assistance of those bullies when we were younger? Do bullies play a role in making us who we are? I think they can be if they just don't get too carried away with their exploits. I believe that some of these bullies just carry things too far.

Maybe a little bullying can be helpful. I think you need to know when to stop.

One last example: When I was in high school there was this football player that always picked on the country boy. They were both about the same size. The football player was always talking loud and in everyone's face. He wasn't a bully to everyone he just seemed to have a problem with this one boy. This went on for months and months. Finally, the football player challenged the boy to a fight. He said to meet him at the football field today after school. All the school knew about it.

Both of the participants showed up. Pretty much everyone was there. Everyone stood around both of them in a big circle. Both the guys were face to face. The football player hit the country boy in the face two times. Blood was pouring out of his mouth. He just stood there with his arms by his side and never moved them to fight back. The country boy just stood and looked at the football player and smiled. The country boy just smiled and walked away. That football player really looked like a jerk to everyone. That football player never bothered that country boy again for some reason. I guess the football player finally realised the country boy didn't consider him a threat or something. I guess if you finally realize your picking doesn't bother someone then why spent all that time and energy if it does not matter?

Here is YOUR activity................

What do you think? Have you ever had a bully? Do you know anyone who had a bully? What did they do? Did they just ignore the bully? I am sure you have some example that is close to you or someone you physically know. How about your parents, relatives or friends? Ask them what they think or if they ever knew of any bullies.

## S u i c i d e

This is one of those topics that nobody likes to talk about. Nobody like to discuss it as it tends to give us as humans hurtful thoughts. Thoughts that make us want to cry. Human entities do not like to cry or show emotion in public in general. Most human entities do not like to put our guard down and let others in our inner circle. It tends to make us feel we are vulnerable. This is because we tend to associate suicide as a parallel with death. Nobody likes to talk about death.

When we hear of suicide we have a want to find out what made that person do such a thing. How did that human entity justify and minimize their place as a human being in a society to do such a task. A task that most usually reaches out and has such an effect on the other human entities are around them especially the ones in their inner circle. The inner circle of our closest relatives and friends. These are generally the ones most effected.

Before I go on I will mention why I mention this topics when we talk about security.

Take this example: Joe is the sole entity at an industrial facility that has a very important job within that facility. One day Joe does not show up for work. This is really unlike Joe. It is difficult to run the daily routines of a facility if Joe is not present. No one at that facility has been cross-trained in what Joe does each day. There really is no listing for the tasks that Joe carries out each day. His work friends call looking for him and there is no answer. After several hours' law enforcement are called to do a safety check on Joe at his house. Law enforcement find Joe deceased. It really does not matter whether Joe died of natural causes or a suicide. The point is that Joe has died. Joe's death has put his company in turmoil. You can pretty much call it a disaster. Joe's death is now a disaster at his company.

It does however, turn out that Joe has been going through a really hard time in his private life. Very few people were aware that Joe recently lost his wife to cancer after 50 years of marriage. This can really play a toll on your mind.

Other than relating this scenario to a disaster at his plant. We can talk about the use for and need of Business Continuity Plans (BCPs) and Disaster Recovery Plans (DRPs) but I want to make this topic more prolific. Here is my premise. Human entities do not like talking about death and or suicide by any means most generally. In my honest opinion that is the main part of the problem! Topics like this need to be talked about more! Topics like this need to be discussed and brought out into the open. Holding these feelings in is a real issue. We know in fact that by all the organizations available in the public, we know that talking helps. There are organizations for alcoholics, drug addicts, parents who have lost children, women who have been molested and or raped, just to mention a few. If talking to others about these things did not matter these organizations would not exist.

Example: Your university professors. If you suddenly drop out of turning in assignments we do not know what is going on with you unless you tell us. We want to know. Maybe there is some way we can help. You don't need to just submit nothing and take an F for a grade if there is some way to change that. It is really up to you. In the end it really is up to you, but you can make others aware of your situation. Why not try at least?

What is the saying "Everything in time shall pass". It does! I am living proof of that! There have been several points in my life where I actually thought of just ending my pain. When I got divorced after 3 months. I wanted to just lay down and die. Why, because I did not know why I was getting divorced, things just didn't make any sense. We had dated for eight years, then married for less than 3 months. Does this make sense to you? I finally, after three years came to several realizations. These realizations made sense and I was curious as to why I had such dire thoughts in the first place. I was glad I did not carry out what I was thinking.

In another example: For the last two years I have been in pain every day I would go home after my classes and cry and scream from the pain inside me. My dogs would just sit and look at me and wonder what I was doing. I would look at them and say to myself that I could not just leave them alone. I had rescued both of them and it was my responsibility to take care of them. Who would take over for them if I was gone? Anyway, after two years of daily pain I finally found a specialist that said he could help my internal issue. I took the chance, had surgery, and this past week was miraculous, I felt better last week than I had in the last two years. If I had ended my life I would not be here writing this today. I guess what I am trying to say is that sometimes our minds can play a sort of trick on us. Our minds are so powerful. With the wrong motivation our minds can twist and turn realities and make us do things that we really did not have a chance to think about.

I have had several friends in my life commit suicide. It is never pleasant. Nothing sad is pleasant. I can attest to that. If you ever have thoughts like I am talking about talk to others around you. Let out what is bothering you. Don't keep it bound up inside you and take over! There are reasons there are myriads of psychologists who seek clients. That is what a psychologist does, they ask questions to you to see your answers and reactions, then they let you know why you think or do the things you do. You would not believe how many human elements need this form of help. You really would not.

I understand why. Sometimes you just need to be made to understand yourself.

Here is YOUR activity................

What are your thoughts? Have you or anyone you know dealt with this topic? Did things get better? Your explanation here is up to you. Do you think talking would help someone in this type of situation? Would talking help? Things happen to all of us. Do you take time to talk to relatives or friends if something is bothering you? Do they talk to you? Are you open to talking to them if they seek you out for advice?

## Last Year

The last year of YOUR attempt at completing a university degree is the most critical!

A Computer Science BS or MS degree is up there with the most difficult degrees as engineering. Programming languages, statistics, high level mathematics, and creative and critical problem solving are the reasoning behind this. If YOU look at other degrees YOU may find a few examples of some of these courses but all-in-all YOU generally will not. If YOU are in one of these programs YOU chose that program the program did not choose YOU! Expect some level of difficulty. If it was a simple and easy prospect the money for completion would not be as high as it is and neither would the positions be so available.

The reason for this particular activity is to give YOU a heads-up of suggestions or really necessities YOU need to review during YOUR final year of studies.

Become involved! This is in addition to YOUR normal course load. Look for projects within YOUR area of study. Talk to other students or professors to see what is available at the time. Each semester may offer different projects. Some of those projects may involve paid stipends. Some of those may involve travel internal and or external of the United States. This is all paid by grants, scholarships, or special funds. It won't cost YOU a penny but it is great experience to put on a resume. Employers look for these things.

How about an internship. It is up to YOU to seek out internships but sometimes professors within a department have links to these. If YOU do a great job for the intern employer they may offer YOU a position when YOU graduate. This happens quite often.

How about getting involved in competitions? These sometimes lead to job offers as well.

Put a resume together. Go to all recruiting events YOU see. Walk around and gather some business cards. Talk to some of the vendors. Ask them questions. That is why they came!

How about certifications or certificates? What are top ones in YOUR proposed area of expertise? Look up companies and see what they recommend for their employees and or applicants. Job advertisements can sometimes tell YOU a lot!

RESEARCH…………..

This course YOU are in this semester is related to cyber security. So, it would make sense for a student enrolled in a cyber security related program and taking a cyber security related course would start to think about things related to security and or cyber security. Right?

This is college, YOUR time going to k-12 classrooms is over. It is time to think like an adult and come to the realizations of an adult. Put YOUR cell phone down and pay attention!

Example: Some employers look for degrees, some experience, some certificates, and some certifications. Some look for a combination of these.

Here is YOUR activity................

Do a little searching here, research. Look at some job advertisements. By now YOU should have an idea what area or specialty YOU see YOURSELF doing as a career.

Find 3 (Three) job advertisements within this state YOU may be interested in after YOU graduate. Answer the following questions for each of the 3.

1. Name of company
2. Brief description of company
3. Location or locations
4. Job title
5. Brief job description
6. Are they looking for: Degree, certifications, certificates, experience
7. Pay
8. Benefits

9. Does this company and or job posting look like something YOU might have interest in after graduation?
10. Would YOU be interested in an internship with this company, COOP, or OJT? Do they offer any of these?

The purpose of this assignment is to help to prepare YOU for YOUR future.

# 12... MY ACTIVITY INSTRUCTIONS

If using any of my activities these are the instructions I use for those specific activities.

## Discussion Instructions

The Discussion activity will consist of:

- Activity will be Zero credit or Full credit.
- Write up and submit a discussion entry for credit points and reply to other student discussion posts.
- Your initial reply should be at minimum <u>200+ words, ideally three paragraphs</u>. Be sure that your post provides a clear and concise response, provides support when needed, and engages your classmates. You will not be able to view other students' posts prior to submitting your own post.
- You must reply to at least <u>two (2) classmates'</u> posts with <u>more than 100 words per reply</u>. These replies must *further the discussion* by providing an alternative point or asking a further question while providing your own perspective. Always be sensitive to the other person's perspective, even if it differs from your own.
- Initial posts are due by 11:59 pm on Wednesday each week. Replies are due by 11:59 pm on Sunday each week.
- Full credit for following directions and accurately completing this activity by the due date.

*Do not use a material submitted by another student or one you have previously submitted in another course! It will be zero credit if submitted.

**The plagiarism program Turnitin will be used to review this assignment for copying and pasting of internet and student material. If you receive a 10% or above score from Turnitin you may receive zero points for this submission. There will be no discussion and no resubmission as you know where you where the work came from before you submitted it.

| **Grading Rubric** | |
|---|---|
| 100% | Directions followed 100% |
| | Correct spelling and grammar |
| | Submitted by due date |
| | No plagiarism |

# Oral/PowerPoint Instructions

The Oral or PowerPoint presentation activity will consist of:

- Activity will be Zero credit or Full credit.
- Title page (Your name, course, semester, "In the News").
- Five (5) pages of content.
- Reference page (You will have a reference page from where you got the story/article).
- Text will be used in this PowerPoint assignment.
- For this credit, you MUST attach your completed PowerPoint as a MS Office Suite PowerPoint.
- NO CLOUD submissions!

- Check ALL spelling and grammar before submission.
- The pages can be as complex as you like or as simple as you like.
- Submissions are due by 11:59 pm on Sunday each week.
- Full credit for following directions and accurately completing this activity by the due date.

*Do not use a material submitted by another student or one you have previously submitted in another course! It will be zero credit if submitted.

**The plagiarism program Turnitin will be used to review this assignment for copying and pasting of internet and student material. If you receive a 10% or above score from Turnitin you may receive zero points for this submission. There will be no discussion and no resubmission as you know where you where the work came from before you submitted it.

| Grading Rubric | |
|---|---|
| 100% | Directions followed 100% |
| | Correct spelling and grammar |
| | Submitted by due date |
| | No plagiarism |

# Thinking Assignment Instructions

The Thinking Assignment activity will consist of:

- Activity will be Zero credit or Full credit.

- The activity is to write up and submit answers to a thinking assignment for credit points.
- Explain with details using a minimum of 200+ words, about 3 paragraphs.
- Use at least APA version 7.
- Cite your textbook and at LEAST one high-quality internet source.
- Be sure that your response is clear and concise and provides adequate support when needed.
- Attach your completed paper as a .doc or .docx file.
- NO CLOUD submissions!
- Check all spelling and grammar before submission.
- This assignment is due by 11:59 pm on Sunday of this week.
- Full credit for following directions and accurately completing this activity by the due date.

*Do not use material or a Thinking Assignment submitted by another student or one you have previously submitted in another course! It will be zero credit if so.

**The plagiarism program Turnitin will be used to review this assignment for copying and pasting of internet and student material. If you receive a 10% or above score from Turnitin you may receive zero points for this submission. There will be no discussion and no resubmission as you know where you where the work came from before you submitted it.

| Grading Rubric ||
|---|---|
| 100% | Directions followed 100% |

| | Correct spelling and grammar |
| --- | --- |
| | Submitted by due date |
| | No plagiarism |

## Essay Instructions

The Essay activity will consist of:

- Activity will be Zero credit or Full credit.
- The activity is to write up and submit a word essay for credit points.
- Explain with details using a minimum of 250-500 words, about 2/3 pages with 12 font.
- Use at least APA version 7.
- Cite your textbook and at LEAST three high-quality internet source.
- Be sure that your response is clear and concise and provides adequate support when needed.
- Attach your completed paper as a .doc or.docx file.
- NO CLOUD submissions!
- Check all spelling and grammar before submission.
- This assignment is due by 11:59 pm on Sunday of this week.
- Full credit for following directions and accurately completing this activity by the due date.

*Do not use material or a written assignment submitted by another student or one you have previously submitted in another course! It will be zero credit if used.

**The plagiarism program Turnitin will be used to review this assignment for copying and pasting of internet and student material. If you receive a 10% or above score from Turnitin you may receive zero points for this submission. There will be no discussion and no resubmission as you know where you where the work came from before you submitted it.

| | **Grading Rubric** |
|---|---|
| 100% | Directions followed 100% |
| | Correct spelling and grammar |
| | Submitted by due date |
| | No plagiarism |

# 13 ... MY OTHER COURSE ACTIVITIES

These are activities I use in courses that may have an intended slant toward either security, cybersecurity, information technology, and or network engineering.

## In the News

We see the news, we read the news, and we hear the news. We get the news on our phones, on our televisions, and on our computers. Sometimes we don't quite realize the relevance on news stories in some of the courses we take throughout our educational careers.

In this Activity/Assignment you will think about topics you read about in this courses and how those topics may relate to things we hear and see in the news. You will point out 1 article in the news that is relative to topics in this course.

## 5 Things I Learned

Some students don't quite realize that they actually have learned something/somethings in their classes. I don't understand how a student can say this when they have passed a course, let alone pass the course with a good grade?

In this Activity/Assignment you will think about what you have learned in this course. You will point out 5 items you can truly say you have learned.

## IT Field Technician

So, you have a job as a field service technician. The company you work for has an SLA (Service Level Agreement) with the maker of computers. This can be any brand from Dell to Toshiba. Through the terms of the SLA you have 12 hours to contact the customer to schedule a visit to resolve (fix) the issue. After you receive the text message from your company that you have a service ticket in your Queue, you login to your account to see what your ticket says. All the ticket says is that it is a Dell workstation and will not turn on. "Service tickets can be VERY vague, and 50% of the time, they are."

So, you call the customer to get more answers. He says, "He knows nothing about computers and can barely turn one on", this is TYPICAL! All he knows is that the brand is a Dell and it is big and silver. This is typical!

If you at least knew the model number of the workstation, you could get online and Google to find out more information about the system you are going to be opening and looking at? Well, as usual, you cannot prepare ahead of time and will have to wait to see the product once you get onsite.

So, you arrive onsite and the customer shows you the workstation. You make some documentation, VERY important! You look on the case and record the brand, the model, and the serial number.

1. Brand:
2. Model:
3. Serial number:

You take out your laptop, log onto the internet and go to the brand website, and lookup the workstation. MOST big brands have these? You may have to make an account? It is free, though. Once you are on the site, you look for "support", generally that is where you look. There should be a location where you can put in the model and the serial number of the workstation or device you are working on. You type in the information and it will come up and give you the factory specifications of the workstation, the warranty information, the date of manufacture, and MANY other bits of information. A few of the things you should document are:

4. Is this still under warranty?
5. What is the date of manufacture or when was it sold?
6. What is the processor?
7. Is there a fan on the processor?
8. Does it have a CD/DVD/Writer/etc.?
9. How much RAM (Random Access Memory) does it have?

WHY? WHY? WHY? Why, do we need all this information? Because, sometimes you can't really trust the customer that he or she is telling you the truth about their system or their knowledge of it? Parts in the system could have been replaced at some point? YOU NEED TO VERIFY THAT YOU ARE WORKING ON

WHAT YOU ARE SUPPOSED TO BE WORKING ON! This covers, YOU! No-one will cover YOU, as much as YOU will!

WHY? If in the SLA that you are to send back the part to get a replacement part under warranty, you send the part back, and it is NOT the correct factory part, YOU will be paying for it or MAY lose your job! YOU must verify everything!

"When you get a call to go to a site and resolve? You will be asked to document what you did and how long it took? There are standards related to time averages to fix issues, and ALL companies know them and use them. This can be a TWO edged sword? On one hand, you can rush and make yourself look like the greatest and quickest technician, and you are well worth the money the company is paying you! Then on the other hand, if you don't resolve the issue and you end up coming back, it MIGHT be on your time and NOT paid! IT IS BEST TO RESOLVE THE ISSUE AS BEST YOU CAN SO YOU DON'T GET A SERVICE CALL TO COME BACK BECAUSE YOU RUSHED AND FORGOT SOMETHING!"

So, you take a physical look at the workstation onsite. First thing you do is make sure it is plugged in. This is number one! If you are a service field tech for very long, you will realize that this is quite a few of your service calls! Or the monitor might NOT be plugged in, or the network may NOT be plugged in, the keyboard and or mouse, etc. So, you have checked all this and you need to open the workstation case. So what are you looking for at this point?

10. Has the case been opened before? You can usually tell? Maybe there is a sticker that needs to be cut or removed? Maybe?
11. Once you open the case, are the devices/components in the case what was on the factory specifications listing?

If all looks well, you can proceed with the troubleshooting. For purposes here, we will NOT be troubleshooting, we will be documenting components inside this workstation. Please provide the information below:

12. What is the brand and model number of the motherboard? It is usually written on it in white?
13. Is this motherboard, proprietary (all or most devices and or cards are built onto the board itself) i.e. sound, video, network, etc.?
14. What type of RAM is used? How many RAM chips are their? According to the specifications on the website are they correct? Is there any RAM built onto the motherboard, other than the RAM chips? What is the total of RAM in the system in Gigabytes?
15. Is the CD/DVD/Writer/etc. the same as in the website specifications? What is it?
16. Is the hard drive what the factory says? Brand and or size? Is the primary hard drive Flash, SATA, or solid state?
17. Is the processor correct? You can remove it and replace it back into its slot. Does it have a fan on it? Does this fan look factory?
18. Does the power supply look factory? What does the website spec say?

19. Are there other devices or cards plugged into the bus slots in the motherboard? Are the slots empty? Are they from the factory according to the website?
20. What type of bus slots are on the motherboard and how many? Are they available or full?
21. Is everything in the case screwed down solidly? You don't want anything just bouncing around.

*Some cases are advertised as "tool less." What is a "tool less" case? A case that you do NOT need any tools to open, close or completely take apart the case or parts within it. Although, you still may need a screwdriver to remove and replace the motherboard, other than that, you generally can remove and or replace anything.

22. Was this case a "tool less" case?

### Pick a Software I

The advent of the internet has opened up the world of research and knowledge vastly. When I first started into college in 2004, the internet was just starting to being used on college campuses. At that time, most school campuses, only allowed students to view certain materials that were available on the internet. It was not open as freely then as it is now. Yes, there is a lot of information on the internet, most is valid and or reliable, however there will always be some that will be false and misleading.

You can imagine, back then, if you were a professor or instructor it could/would be time consuming doing research. Researching most anything would take quite a bit of time. More time than today. Back then, you would have to physically go to libraries, book stores, order magazines, etc. Everything was physical, nothing was virtual as it is today. Today you can order a book or a program and get access to it within minutes or even second. Back then, you would have to call or write a letter to get a subscription, wait for the mail to pick up your request, wait for your check to clear your bank, then wait for your item to come in the mail. It was a lengthy, time consuming process. Students today have it much simpler and can receive gratification almost instantly. This leads us to out Lab Project.

You will take the roll of the professor of this course. You are new at your job, this is your first course. You will research the internet and find a FREE program that you can use in this course. A FREE program related to the Computer Information. FREE means a FREE program, not a program that has a FREE trial, but a FREE program. A program that will assist you in teaching your topic to students. You will research a program, install it, open it, and see if it meets your expectations, then you will document why you chose that program, and the pros and cons you have seen with it. You will write an APA formatted paper giving the specifics. A simple few pages. You can attach your completed paper as a MS Word document or as an Adobe PDF.

Search in Internet?

Research and look at Reviews?

Pick a software?

Install it and take a look at the features?

Why do you Recommend it or NOT?

Document your process and findings.

Submit the Document in Word or PDF.

### Pick a Cell App

Look around at cellular phone applications. For someone to take time and develop an application they had to do that for some reason. I can't imagine just sitting down and spending an unlimited amount of time on something useless. I can see the idea of getting a grade for something simple, but to really spend a quality and quantity amount of time just for a grade I am not so sure. There is more to this than just throwing together a simple PowerPoint presentation, this would be to develop a working model.

Here is YOUR activity................

Search around and find a cell phone application that you think is useless or a sheer waste of time to have. Remember, someone spent time making this.

What is the name of it? Who developed it? Was it free? Is it free? Write up a paragraph about your own opinions of it. Do you feel something about it could be changed, added, or deleted to make it useful? Think about it?

### A Helpful Document

In every field or area within a career there are many documents. A document for this and that, it almost seems exhausting sometimes, the papers we print out, the papers we fill out, the papers we write and turn in. Every step within our existence seems to have a paper trail. "Kill another tree?" We as humans want to save the environment, but we have to stay safe too. Sometimes there is a reason behind the paper document. Sometimes, most generally, we are often not told why we need a document, we are just told to fill it out and keep it for our records. For our records in case someone asks for it later? There may be an instance we could get into trouble if we don't have it or at least a copy of it. We may have to prove something factual. Also, you hear a lot of terms, Problem Solving, Creative Problem Solving, Critical Thinking, and the like. All of these terms have associations and or relationships with each other, although, sometimes they are used in conjunction with each other. This leads us to our Lab Project.

You will come up with a NEW document. A document that you feel could be useful within the area of this course. It can be a document, a spreadsheet, a database, whatever you feel may be of use in the career fields of this course. You will write up and submit an APA formatted prototype of your proposed document in the format of your choice. A few simple pages containing the prototype document, an explanation as to why you chose it, and how it can be helpful. "Maybe there is an existing document currently being used, but is missing critical information?"

AND, let's not forget about Phone Apps? Are there phone applications that exist, or can you think up a NEW one?

## Start a New Account

You will notice that I/We discuss the need to get involved. To get involved during your educational time. There are a lot of things going on at this time, I/We know. That does NOT mean that you have to become content and complacent with how things are? You will be graduating at some point, with other students from around the world. Just think how many Universities/Colleges/Tech Schools there are and how many students graduate each semester? Quite a few! You need to look ahead and prepare to compete with them.

In this activity there will be a list of steps. Step 1, Step 2, Step 3, Step 4, etc.

This Lab Activity will be used in multiple courses I have, as I feel it is important! In a given course you will ONLY complete ONE of the steps. If you have previously completed step ONE in a previous class you will complete step TWO, and so on.

Step ONE: Go to Linked In on the web. Start an account. It is free. Employers from around the world recruit here. They do offer premier accounts that cost money, but that is NOT necessary. I have had a Linked In account for many years and have NEVER needed to pay them anything. This is a great place to meet like-minded people/students as yourself! It is NOT only for employers it is for people and past associates to keep in contact with each other. It is a professional site. If you join, take a screen shot and submit it into this assignments.

Step TWO: If you already have a Linked In account. There is another place you can get a FREE account that I have seen over the years that has been worthwhile. It is similar to Linked In, but is more of a Look, Seek, and Find job site. It is called Career Builder. It is not really a social type of site as Linked In, but employers from around the world look for YOU there! Another is Monster, although I have NOT personally used it, it is a large site for potential employees and employers. If you choose to join one of these, take a screen shot and submit it into this assignments.

Step THREE: If you have previously completed step ONE and TWO, then you will write a nice cover letter. A cover letter introducing you to a potential employer. Do some "Googling" and you will see many examples. If this is your Step, take a screen shot and submit it into this assignments.

Step FOUR: If this is your Step, here is your task. You have been called by a company HR department, they want to meet with you tomorrow. Your task is to come up with 5 solid questions that YOU will ask them. "Every interview I have ever been on, at the end, they always ask "Do you have any questions for me?" This is where you chime in. THEY like QUESTIONS from YOU! THIS shows THEM that you took enough time to do a little research on THEIR company! "It isn't just for you to find out a few things! THIS SHOWS THEM THAT YOU RESEARCHED THEM! This is your time to SHINE!" Don't just sit back and be shy! Show them you went the EXTRA MILE! If this is your Step, take a screen shot and submit it into this assignments.

"Some people are leery of social media sites, and stay away from them. If this is you, we will discuss other options."

## Cell Application I

In some of my courses related to cellular resources and activity I have what I call Cell App Activities. These assignments are made for student s to actually think and to find a way to try and relate something physically and or mentally to the student. Generally I try to make these hands-on if possible.

You can make an App for anything. Start with giving to friends. Friends give to friends, then friends give to other friends. It is as easy as that. Find some little thing that people might like, a little something-something to make them smile, interactive or not. That is all t takes. Stick a $.99 on it and you could be a millionaire almost overnight. How about a bouncing dog, a ring tone from Snoop Dogg, A wake-up call from Taylor Swift, or anything you can think of.

You can even look at ideas already in the marketplace. The problem with company made Apps is they usually have built in advertising constantly pestering the user to buy something else. Who needs pestering? Even if you spend $.99 do you want to be driven insane with bothering ads always popping up or asking some survey question?

As an example, I am not a big fan of drinking water. Instead of setting up timers in my phone for all day I would buy an App that gave me a message every two hours to drink water. All I have ever found have pestered me to death with ads to buy other things. Nothing fancy. A lot of times things are just too fancy or complicated.

For a water drinking App I don't see a need for all the bells and whistles that allow the user to change on the fly all settings that gets too complicated. In education classes when I was younger we were taught a slogan "KISS" Keep It Simple Stupid. I don't see a reason to change settings on the fly. When the App is first installed it asks a few simple questions.

1. Starting time of day for App to start?
2. Ending time of day for App to end?
3. Time intervals during starting and ending times?

All you need. KISS...I would buy it. "This is DOGG, drink some water!"

## Cell Application II

In some of my courses related to cellular resources and activity I have what I call Cell App Activities. These assignments are made for student s to actually think and to find a way to try and relate something physically and or mentally to the student. Generally I try to make these hands-on if possible.

Research and Find a FREE cell phone application maker. You will make a cell phone application that would be useful within this course or useful within a career field relative to this course. It will be either for an Android application or an Apple application. This is a FREE application maker, with NO attached or future necessary nor required subscription! The future subscription CAN be optional. You will make a presentation for the class: Which program you chose; the specifications of the chosen program; what upgrades are available if any; and whether you will be making an Android or Apple application? Are there PRO's and CON's to the program you chose?

Think about the information in the field, what applications for cell phones currently exist if any, what would be helpful in the field, if an application exists could it be tweeked to make it a better more useful application? What application do you propose? You will make a presentation for the class: Make a "story board" naming the application, showing the application and the steps you will make to develop the application.

## Cell Application III

I cannot say how many students come to see me about putting together a phone application. I always get questions like "What app can I make to make a difference" or "I would like to be a millionaire before I am 25, what app can I make" and or "What do you think".

All that being said, in this day and age nothing really stands out and surprises me, when it comes to a human being, what they say and actually what their mind in thinking. Sometimes it is really a stark contrast between the two. Those discussions usually end up with me saying "if you knew what you were going to do in the first place why ask me for my input?"

A few years ago one of my graduate students made a phone app for both platforms, Android and IOS. The student was contacted by a restaurant that had acquired the contract for a local sports stadium to provide food services at events within that stadium. This student did a lot of research as this wasn't an easy task. Anyway, the student met the challenge. She gave us a presentation with all the bells and whistles. Her system worked flawlessly. What she had put together went through multiple trials at live events. So, after all her hard work something happened with the contract and the company went out of business. The fact of the matter was the food offerings were not the typical burgers and dogs at those type of venues, so the customers were not happy at those events for the type of food offered.

This was no fault of the students as her research and implementation was flawless.

It was a rather simple but complex idea. A customer would go to their assigned seat or random. The customer would use their phone app to make an order. The customer would pay for the order through the app. The app would mark the seat or location within the stadium. The order would be hand delivered to their seat or location. All from a phone app and sitting in a location. No more need to stand in line, make an order, wait for the order, and then return to their seat.

I took the student aside and asked her if she had given any right away to the company for her research or was all that development and implementation hers. She said everything was hers. I mentioned that she could take her research and market a package and present to whatever stadium venues she was interested in and at what level and there would most certainly be takers who would want her product. She had no interest and that completed project remains on the shelf.

I have mentioned this idea to multiple students and no takers, so if you have a notion, feel free to develop it, you have my permission. Just send me a postcard when you get to the Bahamas. I'm easy to find.

The first college or university I attended was a small flight school in lower Alabama. My specialty was Avionics and most of my friends were either in Airframe and or Powerplant degrees or Pilot programs. My roommate was a pilot and is currently a captain on a major airline, we still keep in touch. If you know anything about flying you know before you venture to any location through the airspace you complete what is called a "flight plan". A flight plan is a physical plan or document the pilot puts together showing what he proposes to do, where he proposes to go, and when he proposes to land at his/her destination, with stops along the way. When the plan is completed it is put on file.

Why is all this necessary. It is kind of like tracking. I know we have a lot of technologies today, but still it is unreal how many things actually fall through the cracks. What is the old saying "If something can go wrong it will?" Well, sometimes it does. In the world of aviation you need to be as careful as you can as if you leave something to chance, you just might be taking a chance. Whose fault is it then? Well, probably the fault of the pilot as he is the sole person responsible for whatever happens to his/her aircraft. They call it pilot error. Look up past instances with the FAA. You will see the outcome with the vast majority of cases.

Enough about that. What about researching, developing, and implementing a flight plan for land travelers?

How many human beings come up missing within the United States alone each year with no trace? Part of the problem is the majority of persons who disappear are not discovered overdue until at least 24 hours later or even days, weeks, or maybe even months. I don't think law enforcement can really do anything until at least 24 hours after as they want to make sure they do not waste time because Joe Bob just went on a brief jaunt and didn't tell anyone.

What if there was a phone app that tracked your every stop or delay? I projection that the user started with notifications along the way. Notifications could be setup to contact anyone at any time if the user didn't arrive on time as projected in the flight plan. It could be changed on the fly. It would be running in the background and updating every second. Just like having a friend in the driver seat calculating your every move.

If you saved one life would you not have done your job? Would someone pay $9.99 a month for that security and protection? I personally, think we as humans leave too many things to chance. Like I said, send me a postcard and an honorable mention.

# ABOUT THE AUTHOR

I was born in an Appalachian county in central Kentucky. I was once an At-risk, First-time, Underprepared freshman college student, and I would have surely benefited from some gathered information as this.

I received an AS, BS, and MS and was a student worker for my AS and a teaching assistant for my BS and MS degrees. I currently hold 2 undergraduate degrees and 4 graduate degrees and have taken many courses throughout the years. I do not remember having any courses on the topic of retention. Since three of my graduate-level degrees are in Education, I have had many graduate courses directly related to students: Training Materials, Methods, and Evaluations; Creative Problem Solving; Instructional Design; Psycho-educational Assessments; Analysis and Design of Educational and Instructional Systems; Management and Evaluation of Instructional Technology and Distance Education Programs; Instructional Design and Media; Theories of Learning; and Curriculum Articulation, Teaching, Technology, Renewal, and Program Development.

All of those previous graduate courses are directly related to students and their learning. Like I mentioned, my doctorate is in Education not Research. There is a difference, I believe, in both avenues of doctoral programs, but that is another discussion and has been and will be a confusing topic, somewhat possibly a tree branch related to the success of post-secondary college students. I believe successfully taking courses and training directly relating to students and their outcomes has a bearing on how educators relate and come across to students. I believe this to be true. I can't believe anyone in the educational realm is not giving contrary thought to this.

Years later, I am involved in post-secondary education, bringing my ideas, concepts, philosophies, and experiences to my students. Students are the sole reason I do what I do. I will repeat once again: If one single student benefits, I have done my job and fulfilled the purpose of the writing. Currently, I am in the College of Business, Engineering and Technology where I am the Acting Chair and Assistant Professor of the School of Mathematics and Computer Science at Kentucky State University, where my specialties are Cybersecurity, Information Technology, and Network Engineering.

# NOTES

The End

www.ingramcontent.com/pod-product-compliance
Lightning Source LLC
Chambersburg PA
CBHW070847050426
42453CB00012B/2083